THE MUSICIAN'S HANDBOOK

THE MUSICIAN'S HANDBOOK

A practical guide to the law and business of music

William Orobko, LL.B.

SELF-COUNSEL SERIES

International Self-Counsel Press Ltd.
Vancouver   Toronto

Self-Counsel Press Inc.
Seattle

Printed in Canada

Printed in Canada

First edition: July, 1985

Cataloguing in Publication Data:

Orobko, William.
  The musician's handbook

(Self-counsel series)
Bibliography: p. —
ISBN 0-88908-607-9

  1. Music trade — United States. 2. Music trade —
Canada. I. Title. II. Series.
ML3790.O76 1985   780'.23'73   C85-091081-1

SELF-COUNSEL SERIES

International Self-Counsel Press Ltd.
Editorial Office
306 West 25th Street
North Vancouver
British Columbia V7N 2G1
Canada

Self-Counsel Press Inc.
1303 N. Northgate Way
Seattle
Washington, 98133 U.S.A.
(a subsidiary of International
Self-Counsel Press Ltd.)

CONTENTS

LIST OF SAMPLES

To Bronwyn

INTRODUCTION

Your band started to play together three years ago. During the first year, your parents and friends thought you were crazy, and sometimes you agreed with them. After you had jammed in the basement for a year, some of your relatives started to say you were good; after two years, your friends even dropped by to listen. Now *you* are starting to believe that you are good . . . very good.

Over the last few months, you've practiced more than ever before. You've even played in public; the neighborhood high school needed a band for a dance and someone thought of you. You even got paid! It wasn't much, but it was enough to make you feel good. One of the local car clubs has asked your group to play at its next dance, and a couple of other clubs have said they are interested as well. You can cover the Top 40 with your eyes closed. You're pretty sure that this is just the start — there are a lot more places to play and people prepared to pay you.

You are about to hit the road as a professional musician. But how do you start? Where do you go from here?

The first step is to create a business. You probably haven't thought of your music as a business up to now, and, true, it isn't like any other business. You won't be selling insurance, you'll be selling music. You don't have to work from 9 to 5; you can actually have fun when you're working. It's exciting, but nonetheless, it's a business.

Whether you play full-time or part-time, you will now be considered a professional musician. As with any profession, you must acquire a number of new skills that may not seem directly related to music, but are vital to the success of your business.

This book is intended to help you set up your business and to introduce you to the laws that will affect your band and its success. It provides an introduction to music and business law to help you understand and feel comfortable with how the law applies to your band and its day-to-day operations. It will answer enough of your questions about legal matters to help your band function better.

Always remember that a band is a business, and you, just like any other business person, have to understand certain laws and legal mechanisms as well as you understand how to wire your amplifier. No matter what type of music you play, whether it be rhythm and blues, country and western, or Top 40, you must understand the legal implications of running a band. Although law and business may not be your first love, keep in mind that a good basic knowledge of the business aspect of your music will pay off quickly.

Many bands break up because they do not understand the implications of their relationships with each other and with other people in the music business. They fight over contracts, gig dates, and how to split up the profits. This book will help keep you on track when problems occur. It anticipates the problems of running a band and gives you answers, or tells you where you can find them.

It can help you avoid a scenario like this one: Picture the poor rock group miles from home in the parking lot of a small night spot. They were asked to come up and audition, and they thought they had a four-day gig. They travelled all day to get there, spent two hours setting up, and played for four. Then the owner said he didn't like them and wouldn't pay. At 2 a.m. they had to pack their equipment and get out of the club. When they awoke the next morning, they found their equipment had been stolen from their van, and they had a flat tire.

This book can't help you with a flat tire, but it can help your band avoid the other problems faced in this story.

1

GETTING STARTED

The music business, like any other business, has many different facets. There is much more to being in the music business than writing songs or playing in a band. Behind every band or musician is a network of people and organizations that provide the support necessary to anyone in the entertainment field. These behind-the-scenes people include employers, entertainment directors, agents, managers, and lawyers.

The first step in understanding the music business is understanding how these people interact with your band. The person who is the focal point of your group's business affairs will be your business head.

a. YOUR BUSINESS HEAD

A business head is a person who represents the band in all business transactions. At first, you probably won't be able to hire someone for this job, so one of the band members will have to take on the responsibility.

Choose the member of the band who has the most business savvy. The one who enjoys this book the most will probably be your best choice. There is usually at least one member in every group who likes this type of work. This person should have the legal authority to enter into contracts on behalf of the band. His or her signature should be the only one required on contracts. It is very awkward if all the band members have to sign every document related to the band's business.

The business head negotiates and concludes all contracts. Because of the time involved, the business head normally gets an additional slice of the pie. After all, the job takes a lot of time and work. One of your first financial considerations will be how much to pay your business head.

At the very least, the band should pay the business head for out-of-pocket expenses. These include long distance calls, postage, gas, business lunches, and other items that occur on a regular basis. Your business head should keep all receipts to verify expenses.

In some bands, the business head is the least proficient musician. In these cases, no additional payment is made aside from the expenses incurred.

In most groups, however, the business head has equal musical skill. In this case, he or she is entitled to a bit more for the extra time and effort. Some bands pay an hourly rate, and the business head keeps track of the time in addition to any disbursements. This time charge is paid off the top from any money received by the band. Obviously, everyone in the band has to trust the business head to keep track of time honestly.

Unfortunately, keeping track of time is not normally something most musicians like to do. This can lead to bickering within the band over the amount of time taken and how necessary it was. Bands are especially susceptible to this when many hours spent negotiating fail to lead to a paid engagement.

To avoid this kind of bickering, many bands prefer a straight percentage arrangement for paying the business head. After deducting all the costs of the engagement and its negotiations, a percentage is given to the business head from what remains — usually 10%. If the percentage is calculated off the top (i.e., before costs), the percentage is smaller — around 7%. Then, after paying the costs, all members, including the business head, split the remainder equally.

b. EVERYONE IN THE ACT

In the early stages, before a business head has naturally emerged from your group, you might try another route for organizing your business affairs. Everyone can look for gigs, and any member who successfully negotiates one gets an extra slice of the pie. After a while, the one who is most successful at finding jobs may become your business head.

If your band chooses this route, be sure you enforce strict controls and maintain good communication to avoid double bookings.

c. THE CO-OP BAND

Another common arrangement is a co-op band. As with any co-op, the members pool their skills and talents for a common purpose. The business, in whole or in part, is run by the one who likes that sort of work. In an exchange of skills rather than money, the other members take on the remaining necessary duties, or provide additional equipment at no cost.

Though complicated, this arrangement can work well. For example, in a five-person group it might work this way: Sandy has a van and does the driving and provides the van free to the band (but gets gas expenses); Keith is an electronics wizard so he repairs equipment and looks after setting up, sound levels, etc.; Joe is a lover of detail and a hustler who looks after the bookings and takes potential customers out for coffee or lunch; Mike has a P.A. system and provides it free to the band — he also likes to cook so he makes all the meals on the road; Tracy is fussy and is in charge of the details of travel arrangements and security.

Sit down and list the skills, talents, and equipment that the members of your group can provide. Make sure that each is aware of his or her responsibilities. Shuffle things around so that each person has some non-musical responsibility. Write everything down.

Obviously, not all jobs have an equal value. Usually a band splits the profits equally unless there is a great difference in the amount of work done by one band member.

d. PUT IT IN WRITING

The method you choose to pay the business head and reward other skills will depend on what you feel most comfortable with. Whether you pay by time, percentage, or use a co-op method, put it in writing. All of you may agree in the beginning how much your business head will be paid. However, as time passes, and problems develop, memories can fade.

Figure out which method will work best and sit down and write it out. All the members of the band should sign it. This will avoid many problems in the future.

e. BUSINESS MEETINGS

Because the business of a band is important, you should set aside some time each week to review the various business commitments you will have to make. For many bands, the most convenient time is just after or just before rehearsal. However, sometimes emotions can run high during a business meeting. You don't want your playing to be confused with the discussion before the rehearsal; you may not feel up to a business meeting if the rehearsal has been heavy.

The best time is simply when you and the members of the band feel comfortable discussing the business relationship. These meetings don't need to be formal; no one has to take minutes. But it is best to go over what the band is doing and where it wants to be. To avoid general gripe sessions, the business head should prepare a rough agenda for the meeting to keep it on track.

f. WHEN YOUR BAND GROWS

Generally, no band starts out with a full complement of support personnel. Agents, managers, and entertainment directors may be added to your organization as circumstances change and the profits increase. For example, the members of your band will, at first, prepare your promo kit and develop the initial contact with customers. After a while, you may want to use one or more booking agents. When your band achieves some local popularity and wants to spread out, you won't have the time to book engagements yourself. An exclusive agency is desirable when you start to play on a regular basis. After your band starts to play at larger clubs, union membership will be required.

The number of people added on the business side will increase as your band's reputation and receipts grow. The following chapters will help you handle your business affairs until you get to that stage.

2

IT'S A BUSINESS — WHAT TYPE?

Businesses exist to make a profit. That's one of the reasons you and your band got together, isn't it? As the band is a business, it must take on one of the recognized forms of business organization. Your band may be organized as a sole proprietorship, a partnership, or a limited company.

a. SOLE PROPRIETORSHIP

A sole proprietorship is a business owned and controlled by one person. All other members of the band, if it is organized in this fashion, are employees. They work for a specified amount per engagement, per week, or per month. Sometimes, they receive a small percentage in addition to the base salary or a larger percentage in lieu of salary.

The owner of the band pays all salaries or percentages together with all hard costs or disbursements incurred in an engagement. Anything left over goes to the sole proprietor, or owner, as profit. If the costs of the engagement are greater than all expenses, including the salaries or income paid to the members of the band, the sole owner suffers a loss. Obviously, this can't happen too often if the band is to stay in operation.

With this type of organization, the sole owner makes all arrangements for engagements and is the only legal voice for the band. Because the sole owner is responsible for everything that happens, in most circumstances he or she receives a much larger piece of the pie. The band members or employees are limited to income received from their employment contract with the sole owner.

Many of the large stage bands, during the big band era were sole proprietorships. If you played for a band then, chances are you were an employee. You may have been a very well-known employee, but that's all you were. You could be hired or fired depending upon the whims of the owner. Unless there was a bonus arrangement, the amount of money paid per engagement didn't change your salary. On the other hand, a loss at any particular engagement didn't come out of your pocket.

If you want total control of the band, flexibility in changing its members, and the status of having your own name in lights, and if you have the business talent necessary to make such an organization work, this may be the route for you. Remember, everything must be organized by you —from choosing the material, to deciding what engagements to play, to choosing the band members. All decisions are yours alone. As well, remember that a loss in any engagement must come out of your own pocket. You are the captain of the ship and all who sail on it.

Even as a member of a larger group, you can still have your own sole proprietorship. For example, if the group is totally Top 40, and you want to earn extra income by playing at weddings, you can organize a number of sidemen into a group to play for these special engagements. You could be an employee of the main group, but a sole proprietor of your smaller group.

In this arrangement, be careful when working out your costs and expenses. You should also disclose this arrangement to the members of your main group and make sure they don't object. Playing dates, needless to say, should not conflict.

b. PARTNERSHIP

A partnership is two or more people formed for a business purpose. Usually each of the partners is a full partner and has an equal say in decisions and earns an equal percentage of the profits. The losses are also shared equally.

Among themselves, and by written agreement, the partners can vary the partnership format any way they wish. They can adjust percentages and control in any manner acceptable to them. By mutual consent, they can assign various responsibilities to the individual members and set up as many guidelines as they want in order to run the band.

A partnership is probably the most common form of legal organization for any band. More often than not this happens by default. In many cases, the band members never give any thought to organizational concerns — they are too involved in their music. As friends, they have played together for a long time; then they get their first paid engagement and things start to roll. With no formal steps taken, income is split equally among all members of the band. Legally, although nothing is in writing, this is a partnership.

Most jurisdictions have laws governing partnerships. If your group forms a partnership, you should go over the terms of this legislation with a lawyer. The law spells out arrangements that are considered to be part of any partnership. If you don't like the provisions, or if you want to change anything, you need a partnership agreement spelling out your own terms.

For example, most partnership acts say that all partners share the profits and losses equally after costs are paid. But you may already have decided to pay your business head an additional percentage. This arrangement should be written into your partnership agreement. Or you may have adjusted the percentages between the members of your group because some members provide equipment or special skills free of charge. Once again, this can be written into the partnership agreement.

A partnership is normally terminated if *any* of the partners leave or if any new members are added. Once this happens, the old partnership is legally dead and a new one has to be formed to continue business.

In a band, members are joining and leaving all the time — particularly when the band is new. Starting up and dissolving partnerships a few times a year can become time-consuming and expensive. As a result, you should specify in your partnership agreement that the loss of any partner, or the addition of a new partner, will not be sufficient grounds to terminate the partnership. Most legislation does not provide this successor provision, so be sure to include it in your own agreement.

Another basic assumption of most partnership legislation is that any member of the partnership can sign for the group and bind it and all the other partners. This is another aspect you may wish to limit substantially. If one member of the group has a passion for electronic wizardry, he or she might not stop to think of the effect upon the band members before signing a purchase agreement for a mountain of equipment. All the band members may be liable for a bad purchase. You will want some internal control to prevent this and other excesses. Remember, in a partnership, each partner is liable to pay all of the partnership debts.

The partnership agreement for a band, unlike other business partnerships, should cover certain specific aspects of the band's working arrangements. For example, if your band and some of its members are creating songs and original material, you should either specifically include these as part of the partnership agreement, or make them subject to specific arrangements between the contributors and the remaining members of the band.

As well, a band's agreement should outline how new equipment is to be acquired by the band, how members will retire from the partnership, how new members will be added, reasons and methods of terminating a partner, choice of agents and publishers, and any other business aspects of the band's operations.

Other considerations may be:

- Who "owns" the name of the band?

- What happens if two of the five members break off? Who gets to keep the name?

- If the name has a value, how much is paid to the departing members for their interest in the value of the name and other band assets?

9

- What happens to any loans made to the band for equipment purchases?
- Is the departing member relieved from any liability? If so, how?

Because of the flexibility in a partnership agreement and your own desire to cover all the points, expect to pay some legal fees for drawing it up. All of you should sit down with a lawyer and find out what the Partnership Act of your state or province says. After this, you and the band should try to write out all terms of your relationship that are important. When this has been worked out, tell your lawyer what you want, and let him or her add to it or suggest improvements. Unless you can afford it, don't eat up your lawyer's time (and your money) trying to haggle out the various provisions of the partnership agreement in his or her office. That would be expensive, and a waste of time.

Notwithstanding the expense, it would be foolish to proceed with a partnership agreement without involving a lawyer. The law of partnerships is quite complex, particularly when you consider copyright, trademarks, and other matters that may have to be included. A kitchen table agreement might work, but it might also add substantially to your problems.

Your state or province may permit the registration of a partnership along with the partnership name. Ask your lawyer about this. Registration can provide some additional protection for your name prior to obtaining a trademark. Some jurisdictions require registration.

Although it is easy to do, don't fall into a partnership simply because of apathy. Think about it and plan it; work out what the band actually needs and what relationships are most important. Good or bad, your decisions are legally binding.

c. INCORPORATED COMPANY

Most businesses — small, medium, or large — are incorporated companies. Chances are your corner grocery store, the landlord of your apartment, and the company that sells you power and electricity are all corporations. They have presidents, vice-presidents, boards of directors, and all the other paraphernalia that goes along with a company.

You can recognize an incorporated company by its name. Every corporation must have the word Limited, Incorporated, or Corporation, after its name (or the appropriate abbreviations: Ltd., Inc., or Corp.).

Before companies evolved, most businesses were an extended form of partnership. That meant that each member of a business group was liable for all losses the business incurred, as are members of a partnership today. This caused a lot of problems for businesses, and made any business venture quite risky.

Limited companies introduced the notion of limited liability into business. If you incorporate, you are not liable for losses beyond the value of your shares in the company. That is, if your shares cost $10, that's all you lose if things don't work out.

Another unique characteristic of a limited company is that it is not, like a partnership, a collection of equal voices. It is a totally new voice. Legally, a limited company is a person. It is, as lawyers say, a separate legal entity removed from the identity, characteristics, and wallets of its owners.

To take this one step further, the limited company, once incorporated or "born," has almost the same capabilities a person has. It can own or sell property; it can commit crimes and take on debts. Incorporating your group is like adding a member to your band.

The members of a company have a different relationship to each other than do partners. Partners, for example, have an undivided interest in ownership of the partnership property. In a company, the shareholders do not own anything other than their shares in the company. The company itself is deemed to own its own assets. It also takes on its own debts. It pays its own taxes and is liable for its own negligence.

In general, a limited company is much easier to put together and keep running than a partnership. For one thing, the limited company is "immortal." Notwithstanding any changes in its membership, the limited company may continue in existence. Some have been around since the 1600s. The limited company doesn't die; its membership may change but the rest of it is eternal. This can have substantial effect not only on the members of your band but on their families and children, particularly when it comes to copyright and record income.

Shares in a company are much easier to transfer than interests in a partnership. This facilitates the retirement of an old member or the addition of a new one. Since the company owns its name (and probably the band name) as well as any copyrights, trademarks, and other assets the band has acquired, the termination or addition of a band member is much easier; the price to be paid to the departing member for his or her shares is the only consideration. Flexibility of membership is one big advantage to incorporation.

If your band incorporates, chances are the new company formed will own the band name, the rights to any trademark material, and all equipment purchased by the band. If the band has been playing for a while, the old partnership can sell these items to the new company following incorporation. This can result in tax and accounting benefits. The company can make arrangements to "lease" or "rent" from the members of the band any equipment they have that the band wishes to use. For example, Sandy's van can be rented by the company for the purpose of getting to and from an engagement. That means that the van expense is now paid by the company as a hard cost of the engagement and makes the division of profits or income a little easier.

The members of the band obtain their income from the company in a number of different ways. They can be paid a salary as employees of the company, even though they own an interest in it. They can receive a further payment as directors or officers of the company. They also can divide up the profits left over at the end of the year by what is called a dividend. Each method has tax ramifications and the potential for savings.

Social or unemployment insurance, workers' compensation, and other benefits not available to partners may well be available to the members of the band if they are employees of their own company. Your lawyer and accountant can tell you if these advantages are available in your area as fringe benefits to incorporation.

In summary, there are sound business reasons for incorporating. First, it makes the day-to-day operation of the band as a business unit much easier. Second, it can substantially affect the taxes you and the members of the band pay. Third, by using the company, you can avoid many of the other problems that might arise from a partnership and, potentially, some of the liability. In addition, you remain flexible and are recognized as a solid business organization.

If you do decide to incorporate, you may be able to do some, or all, of the paperwork yourself. In most jurisdictions, incorporation is a straightforward procedure that can be accomplished by filling out the appropriate forms, filing them when necessary, and paying the incorporation fee. However, if you want a complicated share structure, or anything out of the ordinary, or if you are unsure of any procedure, you should consult your lawyer immediately and ask for assistance.

d. SPECIAL CONSIDERATIONS OF SETTING UP A COMPANY

1. Shares

There are a lot of things to consider when starting a company, not the least of which is the share structure, or the number and kind of shares.

If the share structure is simple, you and the other members of the band own the same type of shares and the same quantity. However, you may find a more complex arrangement is better. For example, each member of the band can hold a different class of shares. All would be nominally equal, but you can make adjustments for different factors and declare different dividends. This means

13

you can fine tune the payments to take advantage of your tax laws. While each member of the band might be paid the same amount, the fine tuning for tax purposes might see some members take it all in salary while others take their money out as dividends and salaries.

For example, band members with families can split their incomes to cut down on personal taxes. A band member could be paid a salary, and his or her spouse could be paid a dividend by the company. This kind of arrangement can substantially reduce the tax paid on money taken out of the company.

You can also assign certain share classes to different instruments in the band, have a different share class for the song-writing members, or do just about anything else you want with share classes to make the system work best for your band. Lawyers and accountants have a lot of fun with this. What is fun to them can result in substantial savings to you. Check with them about the best way to handle your share structure.

2. Directors and officers of the company

Every company has a board of directors, which sounds rather formal until you remember that your corner grocery store, which is incorporated, also has a board of directors. If your band has five or fewer members, all members can be on the board of directors without it becoming unmanageable. The shareholders elect the board of directors, and the board rules and governs the policy of the company. In a band, this does not have to be elaborate or formal in structure.

Next on the list are the officers who have the duty of running the company on a day by day basis. These include the president, vice-president, secretary, and treasurer. If you wish, every member of the band can be an officer as well. Just add a number of vice-presidents until everyone has a title.

The board of directors appoints or elects the officers from its own ranks. In a large company, these functions are kept separate. In a small company, however, the share-holders are the same people as the board of directors, who in turn are the same as the officers. The five band members might also be employees of the company. Thus, a further hat is added.

For each of the varying roles you have in the company, you can be paid. As a shareholder, you receive dividends. As a director, you receive an honorarium. As an employee and officer, you might receive a salary or wage. All have different tax consequences, which should be checked with your accountant.

If you have organized your band around a sole proprie-torship or if you are a solo act or a duo, don't think you shouldn't incorporate. Chances are you can obtain the same benefits as a larger band. Check it over with your lawyer and accountant, weigh the pros and cons, and then decide. Look at both partnerships and limited companies before you decide on the best organization for your band.

3. Personal guarantees

As mentioned earlier, the main advantage to incorporation is the limited liability. As the company is a separate legal entity, it takes on its own debts. If the company has bought something, none of the shareholders in the company is personally liable to pay the debt. If the business for your band drops off just after you have acquired a mountain of equipment, the company can be sued for payment but not the individual members of the band.

Unfortunately, most creditors figured out a way to get around this a long time ago. Many will ask for your per-sonal guarantee, especially when you are just starting out.

If an equipment supplier or a lender asks you to sign a personal guarantee for your company, and you do so, you waive the protection the company gives you against that creditor. By signing the personal guarantee, if the com-pany doesn't pay, the creditor can go after you or any individual member of the band who has also signed.

Let's say the mountain of equipment you just bought has been outdated by technology. It isn't worth much any more — certainly not what the company owes. The creditor may well decide to sue you or another member of the band because you have some assets. The judgment against you is worth more than the equipment itself, as the creditor can claim anything you own, including your new Corvette. Then you have the hassle of trying to recover from the company or trying to get contributions from the remaining members of the band.

The best solution is never to sign a personal guarantee. But, if you must because a lender insists, make sure you understand all the implications.

4. Signing for the band

In the case of a sole proprietor, only the owner is entitled to sign any business documents. In a partnership, all partners are equally entitled to sign but can restrict this right among themselves in their partnership agreement. The full signing power for a company will be worked out at the time of incorporation. Try to keep it simple.

With a company, it is important to let people know they are dealing with a separate legal entity. This should be reflected in your promo kit and legal agreements, and your bank account should be in the company name. If you are signing for the company, always make sure the company name appears above your signature and that your office with the company (e.g., "president") appears under your name. After all, you want to avoid the personal liability that might otherwise attach to you.

Regardless of the business entity you use for the band, there may be times when you want to delegate signing power for the band to another person — your agent or manager, for example. This is done by a document called a power of attorney. It can be prepared by your lawyer, and it should be limited in both purpose and duration.

Talk over the terms of any power of attorney and understand clearly what you are granting to the person who will sign on your behalf. You don't let many people sign your personal checks, do you? With a power of attorney, you have to be confident that the power will be used as you direct.

5. Shareholders' agreements

The format of a company tends to be rather rigid. Each state or province has a required form that must be used. Because of this, many lawyers recommend that members of a company enter into a shareholders' agreement at the time, or shortly after, the company is incorporated.

A shareholders' agreement is similar to a partnership agreement; the differences are largely technical. The end result combines the advantages of a partnership with the features of a company. But it is more expensive. The details of a shareholders' agreement should be reviewed with your lawyer.

An agreement of this type can provide, for example, that a member who retires from the band must sell his or her shares in the company to the other members of the band or a person selected by them. It can also provide formulas for determining the price of such a sale. This would take into account all of the assets of the band (and the company) and numerous other factors. The agreement will also attempt to provide for arbitration if there is a disagreement among members. It can answer many questions that may arise from the band's operations. It is a way of making your own rules rather than simply following the norms established by the legislation of your particular state or province.

e. COST

The cost of setting up your band as a business will vary depending upon the type of business organization you choose. Just as it is more expensive for you and the other band members to have your performing costumes custom-tailored rather than buying them off the rack, you will pay more for a legal agreement that does not follow a standard format.

Because partnerships are all legally custom-tailored, they tend to be quite expensive. A company, on the other hand, is a fairly standard item in a lawyer's portfolio. You can buy one "off the rack," the way you'd buy a costume. Even with a little bit of alteration, the cost may still be less than a partnership.

Review with your lawyer the cost of both the partnership agreement and incorporation. You might find that incorporation has more benefits and an equal, or lower, cost than the partnership. The more the product has to be custom-tailored to your needs, the more expensive it will be. Remember, though, that this cost will be drawn out over a long period of time — as long as the band continues to operate and play. As a result, and even assuming a five-year span of life for the band, the cost wil be relatively small.

f. COMBINATIONS

You don't have to stick to just one type of organization. For business reasons, several may be combined in any fashion you require. An incorporated piano player may get together with a bass/drum partnership. A corporate band may hire a sole proprietor or a partnership. The different types of business organizations may be combined as you wish to accomplish a specific purpose. Again, if you complicate your business structure in this way, it is wise to review the details with your lawyer.

3

CHOOSING A NAME AND MAKING
IT STICK

A good name can add a certain luster to your band. If well chosen, the name can enhance the band's reputation and provide a hook which will encourage listeners to come and hear you and club owners to hire you.

On a practical basis, the name of your band should do more than simply provide identification; it should convey a sense of the group to your potential audience. It should help create what public relations people call image; it must be distinctive, original, and catchy. The name and your music should stick in the minds of those people who hear your band.

The name should also be protected legally. This chapter will help you do just that.

a. WHAT DO YOU CALL YOUR BAND?

First, do some brainstorming. Of all the names suggested by the band's members, friends and others, are there any that feel right to the group? More than one? Great! Write down all these names on a sheet of paper. Add to the list over time, perhaps while working under a temporary name before you establish a definite reputation. Try to think of a name that is easy to remember and reflects the image of your group.

When you feel the list is complete, or when you have just the right name, check to see if you can adopt and use the name. If another band has already claimed the name, you have to go with your second, third, or fourth choice until you find a name that has not been used by another group.

As with many things mentioned in this book, the amount of checking and the amount of legal protection you obtain through a name depends to a large degree on how the band will evolve. You can spend thousands of dollars in an effort to protect the band's name; but if the band is a local group and wishes to remain so, this is too expensive. On the other hand, if the band intends to play in different states, provinces, or countries, the cost of protecting its name is probably warranted. This is particularly true when you begin recording.

b. DOING IT WITHOUT A LAWYER

No matter how original you think the names on your list are, someone may have used one or all of them before. On your own, with no expense, you can check various publications, such as record catalogues, music lists, and others. The basic idea of this search is to see if any other group has used the same or similar name. Once you find that another group has used your chosen name (or something close to it), cross that name off your list. It is something like looking for a needle in a haystack — but at least there are some maps of the haystack to make life a little easier.

First, in the public library or a book store, you can check various music publications, such as *The Billboard Book of Top 40 Hits — 1955 to Present* (see Bibliography). These lists contain the names of bands who have recorded or are currently recording.

After checking the publications of recording artists, another quick check may be made with the various unions. A letter to each of these unions, either at their head office, or your nearest local, will provide you with a further check. You can also write to The Harry Fox Agency Inc., a mechanical rights agency that has a substantial interest in avoiding conflicting names within the music business (see the Appendix for addresses).

You should, of course, also check with local club owners and potential employers. Many of these will be known to you and will have a good knowledge of the local groups. Shy away from anything that even looks similar to the name of another group in your area.

If your band intends to remain local, chances are you need not do anything more. This type of local search is inexpensive (just the cost of a stamp or two). It gets more expensive and certain legal requirements must be met if you want more protection.

c. NAME PROTECTION

If your band is going to play in more than one city, some name protection can be obtained from your state or province. This protection is limited to the state or province that registers the name you wish to use. For example, if you register your name in Oregon, you will not be protected in California.

On the state or provincial level, there are basically three types of registration. These are:

(a) Registration of the name of a limited company

(b) Registration of a partnership name, business or fictitious name

(c) In the U.S., state trademarks.

Each jurisdiction has specific rules about name registration. You need to look into the regulations in your area.

One of the fringe benefits of incorporation is the additional protection given to your name. If one company has a certain name, no other company in a similar business is permitted to use the same or a confusingly similar name in the same jurisdiction. Legally, you can prevent another band from operating under the same name.

For a small fee (about $10), you can check with the Registrar of Companies to see if the names you have selected have been used before. This is called a name search. It will determine if your selected name is similar or identical to other names used in the past.

If the name search is successful, you can reserve your name to prevent anyone else from using it for the short period of time while you get the incorporation in order. The name search is limited to incorporated groups.

If you form a partnership, you may be able to register your name. Because the regulations differ in every jurisdiction, you should check with your lawyer to determine if

21

registration is possible. Once again, remember that whatever protection is afforded is only for the jurisdiction in which you register.

Even if you have registered your partnership or corporate name in your state or province, you don't have total protection for the name, nor can you assume that you are entitled to use the name or part of if as a trademark (band name) to identify the public performances of the band. For example, another band may have used the same name in another state or province prior to your use, and may have prior rights to the name.

In the United States, many states have their own trademark registry. Once again, check with a lawyer in your area to see whether your state has a trademark registry and, if so, what the procedures are for registration.

If your band is not recording, or is recording only for local labels, name registration at the state or provincial level is as far as you need to go. The expense of proceeding further is too much.

It is important to understand the type of protection you have acquired. If you have thoroughly done your own search, and assuming there are no surprises, you can *probably* hold onto the name, and *possibly* prevent another band from using your name on a local basis. If you register your name, it can be evidence of your priority rights in the name. You can *possibly* prevent use of the same name by another band in your state or province.

However, you cannot prevent a band from using the same name or a similar name when the other band is operating in another state, province, or country. Also, it is possible that you may not be able to hold onto the name of your band if the name you have adopted, at the time you adopted it, was well known. For example, you wouldn't be able to use the name *The Rolling Stones*, nor could you use the name *Dave Clark Five* even if your name is Dave Clark.

d. REGISTERING A TRADEMARK

You should consider registering a trademark at any time you have the money to do it, but particularly if you intend to cross national borders or to record for a widely distributed label. If some time has elapsed between the formation of your band and the time you want to trademark the name, it is advisable to repeat your name check or search. After all, things change. At the time the search was initially done, presumably there was no problem. In the interval (which may be several years or more), a new group may have come on the scene.

A trademark (or service mark in the U.S., when used for a service such as music) is basically a word, phrase or logo used by a business to identify a specific type of product or service. For a band, the service mark (the band name) distinguishes the band's services (music) from those of other bands. If the band name includes a logo, the name and logo together may be copyrighted as a work of art. More often, however, the logo and/or the name are trademarked.

In fact, your trademark lawyer will tell you that both can be done. For example, the name *The Rolling Stones* has been trademarked both with and without their distinctive logo design. In other cases, the logo and name are intertwined. Nonetheless, your name should be trademarked without the logo for additional protection.

1. How to do it

It is very difficult to obtain a trademark on your own. You should seek out a lawyer who specializes in trademarks or, at the very least, use a trademark agent. Normally, a trademark agent or trademark lawyer will be listed in your local Yellow Pages. If not, look in the Yellow Pages of a larger city nearby.

First, your lawyer or trademark agent may advise searching the trademark registry to determine if the name, or a similar one, has been used before and in connection with the same type of service. If a logo is used, it must be drafted in a format acceptable to the appropriate trademark registry. After that, and assuming the name is registrable, your lawyer will prepare a number of forms for your group to sign. The trademark is then registered in either Washington, D.C., or Ottawa, or both. Subsequent registration of the trademark in other countries may follow as your business expands.

Prior to registration, you should affix the symbol "TM" near your name or the logo. This symbol advises others that you regard your name as a trademark. After the trademark has been registered, the standard trademark registration symbol ® can be placed near the logo or the name on each use. It is important to use this symbol, because otherwise you *may* lose the rights to your trademark.

Trademarks or service marks come in two main varieties. The first are words or phrases that are peculiar. For example, a band name like *Znernox* would qualify as a completely new word. Misspelling a word, such as *The Byrds* or *The Beatles*, also comes under the "peculiar" category. This affords better protection than does the second type of trademark, which are common words or expressions. If you fall into the second category, you can give more protection by using a distinctive logo or script in the name (like the group *Chicago* does) or add the name of one of your members to further identify the group.

2. Cost

Registration of a trademark is expensive. You can expect to spend $400 or more obtaining a trademark. Registration also takes a long time — usually more than a year. The benefits however, are quite substantial because registration gives protection across the country. A federal registration in the United States provides protection in all 50 states. In Canada, a federal trademark covers the entire country.

Owning a trademark gives you the right to prevent other people from using your name or logo without your consent on anything which the public might perceive to be linked with your band's services.

Depending on how well known your band is, you also have control, to a limited extent, over spin-off products (e.g., T-shirts, coffee cups, etc.), and can expect to be paid a royalty for the use of your logo on these products.

You can go to court and legally prevent anyone else in the country from using the same name as your band. This is done by what lawyers call an infringement action, which arises when someone else uses or abuses your trademark.

To protect additional products, it is usually advisable to expand your trademark registration to cover the additional items. Your lawyer will try to obtain an injunction to prevent any unauthorized use and get damages — monies that you are paid if someone uses your name for profit without your consent.

The trademark becomes a form of property, something you own and can control. It has a value. You should make sure that its ownership details are spelled out in an agreement. For example, you should specify what is to happen if one or more members leave the band.

The trademark can exist in both the United States and Canada in a common law form, without formal registration. The difference is the effect of registration. A registered trademark is evidence of ownership. Infringement actions are thus made substantially easier. As with copyright, registration of the trademark enhances the value; registration provides a bench mark — it offers positive proof of the registration and the validity of the trademark. It's up to the other side to argue that you don't have those rights.

Finally, if you ever decide to license someone else to make spin-off articles using the name of your band, it is important that you take appropriate steps so that you do not lose the exclusive rights in the name. For instance, in Canada, it is necessary to record the licensee as a registered user at the Trade Marks Office. In the United States, the terms of the license have to be carefully documented in order to preserve your rights in the trademark.

A lot of money can be made from your group name assuming you are successful. It makes sense to protect this name to the fullest degree possible if you wish to exploit it through merchandising at a later date.

Finally, at all stages of name protection, use your name on everything and as much as possible. Use it on posters, letters, cards, and even in the telephone directory. The more you use your name, the better protection you have.

4

PERSONAL REPRESENTATIVES — AGENTS AND MANAGERS

Personal representatives come in all varieties. There are managers, business managers, personal managers, and road managers, to name a few. There are also a variety of booking agents. There are those who are licensed by union and those who are not; there are exclusive and non-exclusive. Lawyers and accountants are also personal representatives, although they are discussed elsewhere in this book.

In the realm of personal representatives, there is a division between agents and managers. The two functions are quite separate from one another. In other words, you might have an agent and a manager — two separate people and two different occupations. In many instances, one person might occupy both positions, but you must keep in mind that such person is actually completing two jobs for you and, as such, is paid for two separate jobs.

An agent is normally one who finds work for your band. A manager, on the other hand, advises and consults with you about your career development. A manager is intensely involved in the band's operations, from artistic decisions to business dealings. Both agents and managers are normally paid by a percentage; both percentages are normally paid "off the top," that is, before any other expenses of the engagement are paid.

Until quite recently, the arrangement between a band and its agent or manager was solely contractual. Whatever rules the parties made among themselves were the rules that governed their relationship. In other words, everything was wide open. Because of abuses that occurred, several unions have developed licensing arrangements for agents. These unions attempt to regulate the basic terms of any contract between an agent and a union band. Some states, notably California and New York, have legislation that governs the relationship between a band and a talent or booking agency. These statutes cover agents only; the contract between you and your manager is totally open and not regulated either by a union or by government.

a. AGENTS

When your band starts off, you and the members of the band are your own agents. You will arrange your own bookings by contacting establishments or groups that may wish to hire you. However, as your band gets busier or better and the members wish to make a full-time career out of music, the need for a talent or booking agency will increase.

An agent provides a link between establishments that use live music and the bands that provide it. This calls for a lot of "know how" and "know who." Your agent must not only understand the music business, he or she must also have a number of contacts within the live music business — sufficient contacts to be able to obtain employment for your group. An agent finds talent for employers to use, and finds engagements and books them for the band. He or she is a link between employers and bands.

Before you enter into any contract with an agent, you should check the agent's reputation among other bands. Ask some questions.

- Has the agent been successful in getting engagements for other bands?
- Have they had a lot of work?
- Has the agent been able to advise them about the nature of the clubs and any potential problems?
- Is the agent honest? Have there ever been problems with "kick-backs"?
- What percentage is charged? Is this normal for your area, or high, or low? If it's high, maybe the agent deserves the additional amount for finding you steady work. If it's low, maybe you won't have much work at all.

The contract between you and your agent should be limited to the engagements that the agent gets for the band — not all gigs that the band gets. If you get an engagement on your own, you shouldn't have to pay a commission. Nor should you have to pay if you get a job from an agent in another town. The commission should not apply to other sources of income, e.g., songs, spinoffs, or anything else. It is advisable to limit the territory of the agent, by provinces, states, or counties, unless he or she is an exclusive agent. A termination clause, so that you can cancel the contract under certain circumstances, is a good idea. It should be triggered by non-performance or inadequate performance.

The next question is whether or not you should use this agent exclusively. If you do, that means that your band can only be booked through that particular agent. If the agent has a large number of contacts, this may be an ideal arrangement. However, if the agent has a limited number of contacts, it can cripple your group. Under an exclusive booking agency arrangement, anyone who wishes to use your band must contact that specific agent.

Alternatively, if you want to use more than one agent, you should ensure that each of the contracts between you and the various agencies employed are non-exclusive. You can have as many non-exclusive agency agreements as you wish, but only one exclusive agency agreement.

A successful booking agent will act for a large number of bands, sometimes 50 or more. As the agent's function is limited to finding bookings for the bands, he or she doesn't have to take much time with each individual band. Depending upon the agent, he or she may or may not wish to offer any additional advice or assistance to the band. Nonetheless, many agents do offer helpful comments about the type of act staged by the band. After all, the more successful and the more saleable the band is, the more frequently the agent is able to book the band and receive a commission.

Remember, any advice an agent offers is given in an attempt to increase both your income *and* the agent's. Listen to the advice carefully, but don't feel you have to act on every suggestion.

1. Union agents

If you are a union band, the relationship between you and your agent is subject to certain regulations imposed by the union. Union bands can only deal with agents who are licensed by the union. They must also sign a contract, the form of which has been approved by the union. Both the American Federation of Music (A.F. of M.) and the American Guild of Variety Artists (AGVA) have developed standard agency agreements for use by their members.

Union agents are under an obligation to find employment for union bands in union clubs, at union scale or above. Union regulations generally provide for a maximum commission — 10% is normal. No commission can reduce the amount paid to the band beneath union scale. That means that the club must pay at least scale plus 10% to hire you.

The contract term between agent and band is also limited. AGVA, for example, provides a maximum term of three years with an option to renew for a further three years. Arbitration is used to settle any disputes between your band and the agent. The recommendations of the A.F. of M. are slightly different; a commission of up to 15% is allowed on steady engagements with 20% being permitted for one night stands.

2. You and your agent

Aside from the percentage, there are other things to negotiate with your agent. Of particular note is whether or not the commission comes off the top or (better for you) after the hard costs of the engagement have been paid. If you are going to deduct hard costs before paying your agent, you must specify what costs this will include.

Your band can negotiate better terms than the agency agreement provides, if you wish. The union only provides minimum standards. For example, you can shorten the term, or provide for percentages less than 10% (if any agent will work for this). You can also provide for minimum performance by the agent. How many one-week engagements, or one-night engagements is the agent obliged to find for you during the course of the year? If the agent fails to meet these minimum standards, you should have the ability to terminate the agreement. If you want to impose other standards on out of town engagements, such as accommodation, meals, and other matters, you should specify these in your agreement.

You have to have a lot of confidence in any agent. You want to make sure that you're booked into clubs where your act will be appreciated. A country and western band playing in a hard rock club will probably not be too successful. If you are on the road, the distance between engagements is important. You don't want to be stranded miles from anywhere with no new engagement in sight.

The relationship with your agent is a two-way street. As mentioned earlier, one of the purposes of the union regulations is to ensure that both parties are kept happy. If the owner pays you directly, rather than through your agent, make sure you pay the agent commission calculated in accordance with your agreement.

Remember that the agent owes a duty to the clubs, as well as to you. Having booked you into the club, your agent may lose credibility with the club owner if you behave in a non-professional manner.

Most groups start off with a number of agents on a non-exclusive basis. At this stage, the agent generally acts more for the clubs than for the band. Indeed, such an agent may have an exclusive agreement with some of the clubs. As your success increases, chances are an agent will want an exclusive agreement with your band. That means that all clubs must come to your agent if they want to book your band. When this happens, the agent then starts to act more for the band than the club.

Either way, remember that one of the agent's functions is to negotiate the booking agreement. He or she normally will try to get more for your band because then the commission will increase as well. This system helps to ensure that an agent will try to get the maximum for your group. Just be sure the agent doesn't lower the price of your group to keep steady work coming in from a particular club. You have to monitor the bottom line very carefully.

3. Government control of agents

Some governments legislate the arrangements between bands and agencies. California and New York are two examples. Check with your lawyer to determine if any legislation exists in your area. If it does, it will probably specify minimum terms for any such agreement (much like the union requirements). Once again, as with the union agreement, you can improve upon the terms, but you can't go below the minimums involved.

If legislation exists in your area, it is paramount. First, you must make sure that your agreement conforms to the legislation; second (if applicable), to the union guidelines; and, third, to your own wishes.

4. Review the agreement

Before you sign an agency agreement, check with your lawyer. He or she will ensure that it complies with the legislation, if any exists. If you are a union band, your lawyer should ensure that it complies with union requirements. Last, but certainly not least, your lawyer should be able to explain the terms of the agreement to you and add provisions, if necessary, to make the agreement satisfactory to you. Never sign an agency agreement without first talking with your lawyer.

5. How to find an agent

As mentioned earlier, you can ask other bands in your area about the abilities and disadvantages of any particular agency. If they have dealt with the agency, they should be able to help you.

Other members of your union, if you belong to one, may have relevant comments. Bearing in mind the somewhat biased nature of their comments, you could also check with various clubs in your area to see how they view the reputation of your prospective agent.

Once you find one or two that seem to fit the bill, send them a copy of your promo kit with your demo. Some agencies like a cassette of a live, uncut performance, others simply want a copy of your best material. Most will want to see an actual performance. In any event, your promo kit may kindle some interest. Some agents try to review new acts by visiting clubs in their area.

6. Your agent as a manager

Although an agent and a manager perform different jobs, sometimes one person serves as both.

If you have a very good relationship with your agent and feel that he or she can occupy both roles — great! Perhaps your agent has offered good advice about the band's act. This indicates an interest in the band's management beyond the role normally served by an agent. You might wish to expand the relationship to include the manager's functions.

Obviously, a person doesn't work for nothing, nor do they do two jobs for the price of one. If your agent has agreed to act as your manager, you should expect to increase the pay. The amount can be freely negotiated or, once again, be subject to union regulation.

In the A.F. of M., for example, an agent who also acts as a manager is entitled to an additional 5% over the normal agent's commission. The total commission payable to your agent/manager is thus between 20% and 25% depending upon the type of engagement. If only 5% comes from the management function, the remainder comes from the function as an agent.

Even if you are signing outside of union regulations, you should check over the A.F. of M. "green form" called *Booking/Personal Management Agreement*. It provides a useful guide; you can obtain a copy by writing directly to the A.F. of M. (see address in Appendix).

You will not want to enter into this relationship until you have established a large amount of confidence in your agent. The relationship with a manager is much more personal than that with an agent, and you may find that your agent is great as an agent but terrible as a manager. Many performers would also argue that two people, even though more expensive, do a better job. There is a certain dynamic relationship that can only be obtained by two people using their best talents to assist and encourage the band.

b. MANAGERS

An agent will act for 50 bands or more; a manager will probably act for no more than 4 to 8 bands. The work of a manager is far more intensive. A personal manager for your band will provide a variety of services ranging from artistic advice to business decisions.

Of all the unions involved in music, only the A.F. of M. has tried to regulate or provide sample contracts for managers. But other unions, as well as the A.F. of M., have tried to establish guidelines for the manager's function. Let's look at the three basic ways that a manager can assist your band.

1. Artistic expertise

The first field of expertise concerns the artistic side of the band — the actual performances and recordings. Your manager should be versed in the music business well enough to advise you about the choice of material, the way in which such material is presented, the type of costumes, and the balance between original and non-original material — even down to the choice or need for additional instrumentation or vocalists.

A manager is almost like having another person in your band. He or she should know what type of act is successful in your area and be in tune with the music business enough to understand and anticipate shifts in pattern. This can give a slightly different perspective to the band's artistic talents. Your band has probably played together for quite some time, but in some isolation. While you may know what you can play well, you don't necessarily know what will sell well. The manager should attempt to blend the band's talents into the mainstream of marketable products without destroying your integrity as musicians. If you think that sounds difficult, it is.

2. Business expertise

The manager has to be able to market the abilities and talents of the band to the public. Like the agent, the manager has to know a number of people in the music business. But beyond that, a manager's job is to guide the band through the maze of the music business to the most successful result.

Timing is critical. You don't want to play too big an engagement before you are ready for it. The manager should be able to recognize potential difficulties or dangers represented by any engagement, and plot these engagements to ensure that the band's reputation increases over time. While the agent's goal is perhaps short term, the manager's goal should be long term. The members of the band and the manager should agree on the end result of their relationship. Does the band wish to record? Does it wish to travel? Do you want to become the best group in your area, but not record? Discuss where you wish to be in a few years to assist your manager connecting present success with future goals.

3. When to hire a manager

The acquisition of a personal manager is usually done much later than the acquisition of an agent. You would normally not require a manager until the band has developed a strong reputation and is "going places."

Nonetheless, there have been cases with certain managers having phenomenal results with a young band; *The Beatles* are one example. After all, the manager doesn't have to worry about performing. He or she can direct any talents to adding thrust to the band's natural momentum.

4. Your manager's function

The A.F. of M. guidelines provide for five basic functions of a manager: the selection of materials, publicity and public relations, the adoption of a proper format to best present the band's talents, the selection of booking agents, and advising on the type of employment the band should accept keeping in mind the end benefit to the band's career.

Many successful performers have relied strongly upon their managers. The closeness of this relationship demands that you like your manager and get along together well. You have to get along with your manager just as you have to get along with other members of the band.

5. The cost

This help doesn't come cheaply. As with an agent, the manager is paid on commission or by percentage. This payment comes, however, from all activities of the band including merchandise, spinoffs, engagements, and just about anything else the band does that produces money. The manager takes a slice from all of these things because he or she is pivotal in arranging for all of them. The percentage generally varies from 10% to 50%, and sometimes works on a sliding scale.

Any contract between you and a manager must be carefully looked over by a lawyer. It should provide a description of what the manager is to do and a full outline of responsibilities. The percentage the manager obtains should be specified and detailed as to how the percentage is determined (e.g., off the top, or after expenses). The contract should provide for arbitration in the event of disagreement and termination in the event of total dissatisfaction. Also, decide what expenses the manager can incur on behalf of the band. Should he or she have power of attorney? Check the details with your lawyer.

Probably no relationship in the music industry is closer than that of a band and its personal manager. It is like a marriage. Unfortunately, the dissolution of this relationship can be just as bad as, if not worse than, a divorce. Even though your manager may oversee legal arrangements after being hired, you should check out your management agreement with your own lawyer independently.

6. Lawyers and accountants as managers

Some groups use their lawyer or accountant as a manager and it works well. However, for others, this arrangement has had disastrous consequences.

One of the difficulties in combining these functions is the loss of independence — not for you, but for the lawyer or accountant. Both lawyers and accountants seem to give their best advice when they are uninvolved. If their interests are directly linked with that of the band, their perspective, naturally enough, gets somewhat distorted.

A lawyer or accountant may have strong business skills, but they are less likely to provide the artistic advice you seek. Be careful before combining professional functions. Proceed with this arrangement only if the personal relationship is strong.

c. BUSINESS MANAGERS

Even when you have hired an agent and a manager, there may still be further need as the band increases its bookings and profitability to add a business manager. Often the band's accountant becomes it business manager. Some managers take on this job as an additional role. Rather than hire a separate business manager, the manager may perform this function as well.

The business manager oversees all administration involved in the band's activities. The nitty-gritty of accounting, legal work, and other services is funnelled through the business manager. In other instances, a business manager can advise the band on investments or other business opportunities. The sale of your logo on certain items is one example. In this role, the business manager would oversee road trips, hire and fire roadies, arrange for equipment acquisitions and financing, and anything else.

d. THE CHAIN OF COMMAND

If all the people employed by the band report directly to the band, there won't be time for much else. The band must establish a chain of command to limit the input from various professional advisors.

Certainly, the closest relationship will be with your manager. Your agent should deal directly with your manager, and not with the band. The band should have direct dealings with its accountant and lawyer on a regular basis, but routine matters may be channeled through your manager. The same applies to the business manager, the road manager, or others. Promoters and other parties would normally deal only with the manager, not the band. It pays to establish some guidelines in this area so you maintain enough time to work on your music without losing control of your business.

The full cost of all these services is extremely high. No band would start off with all of them. Rather, it is usually done in progressive steps. At each stage, services performed for the band are increased and so too is the cost. Elevate the band to the next level only when you can either afford the service or the addition of the service will result in substantially increased income.

5

LAWYERS AND ACCOUNTANTS

a. HOW TO FIND A LAWYER

Unfortunately, there are relatively few lawyers who practice in the field of entertainment law, of which music law forms a part. It is a comparatively new and specialized area and, therefore, not many lawyers are familiar with it.

If you are in a large city, the chances of finding this rare beast are a bit better. In some areas, lawyers are permitted to list their preferred areas of practice or specialties in the Yellow Pages of the telephone directory. Look for someone who lists a preferred area as entertainment law, music law, or copyright. This will get you close to the area.

Depending upon where you live, there may also be other publications available in which lawyers are permitted to advertise their specialties. *Music West*, published in Vancouver, British Columbia by Reel West Productions Inc., lists a number of different skills involved in the music business. Included among these are legal services. If such a publication exists in your area, check it over and limit your search to those lawyers who have shown the interest to place their names in this type of publication. They obviously want your type of work!

You can also ask other bands, publishers, agents, and other people in the music business for the names of their lawyers and whether or not such lawyers provide good service.

1. The first meetings

You should look for a lawyer who you and the other members of the band can relate to. You don't have to like your lawyer; you don't even have to go for lunch with him or her. But you do have to respect your lawyer's opinion when legal questions are raised.

Many lawyers have a small consulting fee for the first meeting. Some have no fee at all for an initial interview. Call up, make an appointment, meet with him or her, and draw your own conclusions. Meet with two or three before you make up your mind.

As you want a long-term relationship with your lawyer, your initial meeting should be the testing ground. Throw out some jargon. Does the lawyer understand what an amplifier is? When you refer to *Billboard* or *Cashbox*, does he or she nod in comprehension or look vaguely confused. Ask if he or she has other clients in the entertainment business — and, in particular, in the music business. Don't be bashful.

You should have enough confidence in your lawyer to rely upon the advice for all matters concerning the business of the band. Note that your lawyer should give *advice*; your lawyer will not, and should not, make final decisions. Those are yours to determine. It is up to your lawyer to interpret the legal jargon contained in an engagement or recording contract and explain it to you in an understandable fashion. It is up to your lawyer to suggest changes and give reasons why such changes should be made, but you make the decisions.

2. Fees

Once you have found a lawyer and feel comfortable with the relationship, prepare yourself for the fee that will be charged. This fee will be based on a number of factors. It will depend upon the time taken (normally the first consideration), the expertise of the lawyer (sometimes measured by the length of time in practice), the amount of money at stake, the complexity of the issues, and just about any other factor that appears relevant. You will also be expected to pay disbursements. For example, if your lawyer buys you lunch, it will probably show up on your bill. Make it easier for yourself and pay for the lunch at the time.

You should expect to pay for legal research, but not a legal education. This is one reason for selecting a lawyer who already has some knowledge of entertainment law, and who is reliant upon the research simply to narrow down a point. A lawyer who is not familiar with the field, and who may charge less on an hourly basis for services, may spend a lot of hours attempting to learn something that should have been learned in law school.

Naturally, you want to know what fees are involved. Check with your lawyer and be specific. How much is charged for time, and how much is charged for telephone advice? The two rates may differ somewhat.

Remember, much of the work is measured by a time yardstick. You are entitled to know how this yardstick is made and what measurements are applied.

After you know the costs, don't hesitate to use the services your lawyer can provide. If you do have doubts about a particular engagement contract and, more particularly, a major contract, it is worth the expense to have your lawyer review it. He or she has probably read a number of these documents before and, as a result, can draw upon past experience to suggest changes that will improve the situation for you and your band.

For a lawyer, nothing is better financially than trying to sort out a thorny problem after it has grown. It's cheaper by far to get some quick advice before a major problem develops. Your bill will be higher if you wait until the problem has tied itself up in knots. A small bill at the start may well save a large bill after a protracted legal action.

Legal fees are not cheap. What makes it worse is they must be paid regardless of how much you earn under a particular contract. Let's say your lawyer's bill is $500 to review a particular agreement for you. Unfortunately, the agreement doesn't work and you receive only $5 from it. Obviously, this can hurt the band's finances if it happens too often.

One way of avoiding this is to give your lawyer a percentage, as you would your manager and agent. Be forewarned, though, that most lawyers don't want this arrangement because they take a chance on getting paid only if you win. However, a percentage is definitely something to discuss with your lawyer if you are worried about fees.

If you are lucky, and if the lawyer thinks that yours will be a successful group, he or she may agree to take a percentage of your gross income instead of charging you normal fees for the work involved. From the lawyer's point of view, this represents a risk. After all, he or she may not get paid if you don't perform up to expectations. As a result, the amount of money received under the percentage arrangement (for taking a risk) is much higher than if you were billed for the work as it was being done. On the other hand, from your point of view, you don't have to pay the lawyer until you do have income. As with most things, the sword cuts both ways. If you can afford the fee, pay it. It will save you money. If you can't, see if you can work out a percentage arrangement.

Any percentage arrangement with your lawyer should be in writing. Your lawyer will probably insist upon this. From your point of view, the same rules apply to this contract as to the arrangement with your manager. You need to have the contract reviewed by a lawyer. But, obviously, your lawyer isn't the one to do this. Pay another lawyer to simply go over the proposed agreement between your main lawyer and your band before you sign it. In some areas, this type of arrangement has to be executed by a client in the presence of another lawyer.

If you have agreed to a percentage arrangement, your lawyer will probably bill you only for the disbursements incurred, or the money actually paid out on your behalf. This includes registration fees and other similar types of expenses.

On the other hand, as you don't have to worry about the time clock, you can call your lawyer more frequently and be less hesitant about obtaining advice on any particular deal.

3. Retainers

Lawyers like retainers. A retainer is a sum of money you pay to your lawyer in advance of any work. The lawyer places your money in a trust account, does work for you, and takes the amount of the bill from the trust account. That way, your lawyer is sure of payment, which is a nice feeling.

Another form of retainer is also sometimes used. You pay the retainer simply to keep the lawyer on your side. In addition, your lawyer bills for all work.

The final retainer arrangement is not used often, but you may run into it. A lawyer may establish an annual fee for all work he or she does for you (subject to certain exclusions) and bill you monthly or quarterly for a portion of this annual amount. This type of agreement should be reviewed carefully with another impartial lawyer.

4. When to use your lawyer
An easy rule would be: don't sign anything without having your lawyer review it. Unfortunately, this luxury is one that most bands can't afford.

Have your lawyer review all major documents: your contract with your agent, manager, record company, and other big deals. These contracts are unique so each will be different. Common sense will tell you when you need this type of assistance.

Other contracts tend to be standard. Your twenty-fifth engagement contract will probably not be that much different than your first. With this type of contract, you may wish to have your lawyer review the first and second with you, but after that you can fly on your own. This would also apply to copyright registration or other routine, standard, and repetitive procedures.

You will also want to use your lawyer to draw up your partnership agreement and incorporation papers if there are any complications.

The best rule to go by is to consult your lawyer whenever you are unsure of anything, or whenever large amounts of money are involved.

5. Conflicts

Don't be surprised if your lawyer advises from time to time that each of you in the band should seek your own separate legal advice. Lawyers are often confronted with conflicts of interest. Simply, this means that a lawyer cannot act for two or more parties in the same transaction who have, or who might have, conflicting interests. For example, if your lawyer drafts a partnership agreement for the band, it would be natural to suggest that only one member of the band sign the agreement in the presence of the lawyer. The other members would have to sign in front of other lawyers in other firms to obtain independent legal advice. Not only does this protect all parties, it also protects the lawyer. After all, if your lawyer isn't smart enough to protect his or her own interests, how will you be protected?

For the same reason, you and your manager or agent will need separate lawyers.

6. Keeping your lawyer posted

Lawyers tend to need some gentle care and feeding. A business lunch or supper can sometimes be the best way of keeping your lawyer up to date on your group without having to pay for it. Generally, the better a lawyer understands your particular group with its own particular and somewhat peculiar interests, the better he or she is able to advise you whenever you have problems.

Most lawyers delight in getting an invitation from their client for lunch. For some reason, the costly time clock may not tick during lunch hours. Use this time not to pick your lawyer's brains, but to talk about your band and to build up understanding, which can lead to better rapport.

b. ACCOUNTANTS

Accountants talk a strange language. Perhaps because they deal with numbers all the time, it seems that they can't communicate with other people save by numbers. Nonetheless, you'd better get used to it because if you are successful, your accountant will be very important to your band.

Your accountant will be your major ally when it comes to income taxes. The tax laws say that you don't have to pay the government any more than the law says you must. Unfortunately, the *method* by which you do things can have a dramatic effect on how much tax you pay. For example, whether you lease or buy the van for your band, will have different tax consequences. So, too, will other equipment purchases. Incorporation will have a substantial tax effect on the members of the band.

You want an accountant who knows these rules and who can advise you as to how to organize things so you pay the least amount of tax. If the government has its hand in your pocket, you want them to take as little as the law allows. No business, even your band, should be (or can afford to be) without an accountant.

Finding an accountant is almost as difficult as finding a lawyer. Once again, you can start in the Yellow Pages. Unfortunately, few accountants (even fewer than lawyers) advertise a specialty in the entertainment area. Your agent or manager will probably know an accountant; other bands may also deal with an accountant and be prepared to recommend one to you.

After you have established the initial contact, follow the same rules as discussed in chapter 5 concerning lawyers. As with lawyers, your relationship with your accountant is a long-term affair. It is important that you get along and, particularly, that your accountant understands the business you are in.

If you are into songwriting, you will also want an accountant who can review the statements you receive from your publisher and performing rights organization to make sure you are getting all the money you deserve, and on time.

When you look for an accountant, you may be confused by the different names they have. In the U.S., they are known as Certified Public Accountants, or C.P.A.s. In Canada, the equivalent term is Chartered Accountants, or C.A.s. These accountants generally are the most qualified accountants you can find. In Canada, there are also Certified General Accountants, or C.G.A.s, who are also well-qualified, but who go through a less rigorous training period.

Many accountants also provide basic bookkeeping services for their clients. This involves giving your accountant your financial records (normally once a month) and having them checked to make sure you haven't made a mistake. This standard bookkeeping function can be done at less expense by a qualified bookkeeper. There are a lot of bookkeepers, but you want to make sure you hire one with a good reputation and who charges a reasonable amount.

The term bookkeeper covers a number of people, both trained and untrained, who prepare the basic financial information for your accountant to play with. Normally, they do not prepare profit and loss statements (which tell you how much the band has made or lost in the given time period) or the like; they just add up the material you give them. Bookkeepers add and subtract; accountants juggle.

6

KEEPING TRACK — BUSINESS RECORDS

Any business has to keep track of its expenses (money spent), and its income (money received). In addition to these basic financial records, other records and files must be kept to keep track of important documents and other necessary matters. As your band is a business, you should do the same. Indeed, insofar as the financial records are concerned, you *must* do the same.

Some discipline is needed here. You can't simply let every member of the band take care of the various components. Your files have to be kept in one location and subject to some form of organization. Your business head is probably in the best position to do this. Whether the records are kept at your business manager's home, with your agent, or with your lawyer, or somewhere else, is immaterial. But they must be kept in one place where you can have access to them, and they must be kept up-to-date.

a. NON-FINANCIAL RECORDS

A band does not need a sophisticated filing system, but it does need *some* system. At its simplest, all you need is a set of file folders where you can place, and later find, important documents. For example, once you prepare the band's inventory, you should keep it where you can get your hands on it. Keep the original and one or two copies in a separate file marked "Inventory." You can then grab on to it, update it, and amend it with relative ease. To redo the inventory every time you need it, when you can't remember where it is, would be a thankless exercise.

Receipts for various pieces of equipment should also be filed. Set up a separate file for each piece of equipment or equipment rental, clearly marked in a manner that makes it easy to find when you need it.

You will also want to keep track of all engagement contracts. This will require yet another file. Union or guild membership, performing rights organizations, and other membership forms should be kept in separate files under the name of the appropriate organization or guild. Tuck all correspondence to and from guild or association into the same file where you can find it if you need it.

Any internal agreements within the band should be kept on file, including the band's partnership agreement, or incorporation documents. Another file might represent correspondence to and from your lawyer; yet another for your accountant.

For most bands, the only element of sophistication needed is some way of grouping the files. Fortunately, file folders come in a number of colors. Pick out one color for memberships, another color for equipment, and so on. Place the files in alphabetical order, by subject, or anyway you like.

Whatever order you employ should be designed to assist you in obtaining information when you need it. It doesn't have to be complex, but there should be "a place for everything and everything in its place." If this sounds simplistic and regimented, try and think of the amount of time such a system will save you when you need the information. Nothing is more frustrating than sifting through magazines, papers, documents, and miscellaneous invoices trying to find something you need just prior to a road trip. By taking the time to set up a system in the early stages, you can save considerable time and respond more professionally to letters you receive when you must.

Perhaps a relative or friend of a member has some office experience. If this is the case, you are in luck. Ask this person to set up a filing system for you if you have any doubt as to what you require.

The files for a band just starting up would probably fit in a large box, so you don't need to purchase a filing cabinet at this stage.

b. FINANCIAL RECORDS

Someone has to keep track of the numbers to feed to your accountant. Unless your agent offers to provide this service, chances are a member of your band will have to do it! Once things get going, your bookkeeper can take over. For now, your business head is probably in the best position to take care of this.

The first rule of band accounting is simple — *save everything*. Whenever you buy something for the band, keep the receipt. Identify it in some fashion and file it away. This applies not only to equipment purchases and the like but also to meals on the road, gasoline purchases, accommodation, and everything you pay for that is a proper and recognized expense of the band's operations. If you are not sure whether something is a proper and recognized expense, keep the receipt, invoice, or whatever until you can check with your accountant.

In addition, if you pay for any items out of your own pocket, mark it down in a small book that you keep permanently in a convenient location. Any expenses that you pay personally should be reimbursed from the band's revenues. Try to get in the habit of marking each invoice, sales slip, or other similar item with the nature of the item or, in the case of a business lunch or coffee, the name of the person with whom you met. Make sure a date and place are on the receipt. Develop some organized method of collecting all of these little slips of paper to verify the expenditures for tax purposes. Even a 60¢ cup of coffee becomes a business deduction if you bought it for the owner of a club where you were seeking an engagement.

You have to find a method of saving all these little pieces of paper. Perhaps the easiest is a simple envelope system. Buy a stack of 12 envelopes and you'll have enough for the year. Any receipt for a given month is placed in the appropriate envelope and the envelopes themselves are kept in a file. Don't lose these envelopes!

The expenses, as evidenced by your receipts, and a record of all income, have to find their way into a ledger. A ledger is simply a book that records all expenses and all income or, put another way, what the band owes and owns. Your bookkeeper or accountant will be able to advise you as to how this is set up and how to keep track on a monthly basis. The ledger doesn't have to be very complicated for a band, but it does have to be maintained. This is easier done on a monthly basis, not in a great rush at the end of the year when memories have faded.

Don't ever take your band ledger on the road with you. It should remain with your other files and records in a safe place. Even if this safe place is simply a cardboard box in the closet of your bedroom, all of these records should be kept together and not scattered halfway across town without good purpose. When you are on the road, you need another safe place for all the receipts you gather and other similar items. A large manila envelope tucked into the glove compartment of your van will probably do. As long as you have some place to temporarily store these items before they are placed in the band's files, you should be okay.

After you or your bookkeeper has prepared all this material, it goes to your accountant on a yearly basis. From this material, your accountant will prepare a document known as a financial statement. This document is the basis of your tax payment. It contains a profit and loss statement, a balance as of a particular date, and other financial information. This is where the tax aspects come up. Depreciation, capital gains, income, and just about everything else gets taken care of in this particular document. The first few times you see one, it won't make much sense, so have your accountant take the time to slowly review the first one or two with you. Remember, the accountant is costing you a lot of money. So, too, are the taxes. Try as best you can to understand the processes involved.

Because the laws of the United States and Canada are substantially different, and so complex, there will be no attempt made in this book to explain the income tax law as it applies to your band. This is best left to your accountant. Suffice it to say, the bottom line is that you pay tax on what you get and if you don't, you're in a lot of trouble.

c. BANK RECORDS

As soon as your band starts off as a business, whether it be a proprietorship, partnership, or limited company, you should establish a separate bank account in the band's name. Don't fall into the trap of using your own bank account or that of another member of the band. After a very short time it will become very difficult to separate your expenses from those of the band. Set up a new bank account right from the start to make things easier.

Although it can get difficult when you are on the road and are paid in cash, all money you receive from the band's business should be deposited into this account. If you are on the road and can't make a deposit, write down how much you were paid (some employers will even insist upon a receipt) and if you divvy up the cash before you get home, write down who got what. As money tends to cause a lot of problems, you may even get a receipt from each band member as to how much he or she received.

All expenses you pay should be paid by check from this account, if possible. Obviously, you won't be able to use a check for a 60¢ cup of coffee in a small diner, but where possible, avoid paying in cash.

Checks should be used for all major purchases or all items that are paid from invoices received, and the number of the check recorded. Just about every bank will give you a book to keep track of the checks you write. Aside from the number of the check, you should record its date and the person to whom it is directed. Keep a running balance in this book, to let you know how much you have left in the bank account. You also enter your deposits in this book. Not very difficult to do, but very awkward if you haven't kept track in a reasonable fashion.

To cover the small expenses that may arise on the road or in town, set up a petty cash system. Each of you can have a small amount of cash to use for band business. As you spend it, get receipts for everything and mark them down in the book you carry for such purposes. When all the money is spent, the receipts are turned in to the band's files and a new amount of petty cash can be issued to you by check from the band's bank account. Your accountant can help you set up an efficient petty cash system.

Once you establish a bank account, someone has to have authority to sign checks. If the band is a sole proprietorship, the sole owner will do this. If it is a partnership, any one of the partners can technically sign the checks. However, you can also limit this power to sign checks any way you wish. For example, you may want two members of the band to sign for all checks. What works best will depend upon the band itself. If you have incorporated, a director or anyone designated by the band can sign the checks. Work out who will sign and then complete all necessary bank forms to make sure that what you want is what happens.

There is nothing wrong with paying out the cash to the members of the band just after it is received. But you should follow a few simple and basic rules. The first is to hold back enough to deposit into your bank account when you get home so you can cover the other band expenses that built up during your absence. The next simple rule is to keep track of who got what and record this somewhere to give to your bookkeeper. The money you take home to deposit into the account plus the total of all receipts should equal the amount you were paid for the engagement. It can then be properly recorded by your bookkeeper or business head in the band's ledger.

In some instances, your contract with your employer will give one rate of pay, but you will receive a different amount. This may be done for a number of reasons, not the least of which is to avoid certain union requirements and border hassles when you are playing for less than scale. But if your contract gives a higher amount than you are paid, and you don't record how much you actually receive, the tax department can tax you on the higher amount. Write down the amount you actually received so you can justify the lower figure.

d. EMPLOYEE RECORDS

If you have incorporated, you and the other members of the band are employees of the band. If you hire a sound technician or other roadies to accompany you on your trips, you may have other employees. As an employer, the band is obliged, like any other employer, to make certain deductions from its employees' paychecks. Income tax, social security or unemployment insurance, and other similar deductions must be made. Your accountant will go over the deductions that are necessary. The government supplies a handy pamphlet that explains how to calculate these deductions. The calculations are rather simple but must be followed on a month-to-month basis for all employees. The employee payroll deductions must be paid to the government by a specified time each month. Failure to do so can result in a lot of trouble. Accurate records must be kept of all this information.

Your roadies may be "independent contractors" (as you are with the clubs), in which case you pay them the gross amount of their salary and they are responsible for making their own tax payments. This is fine, but it can create difficulties. If your roadie is employed for more than a very short period of time, the government will say (regardless of what your agreement is) that he or she is an employee. After a year or two, you could find yourself held responsible for the tax payments that weren't made, in addition to the money you have already paid and that the roadie has spent. Take the advice of your accountant on this matter.

Some people are tempted to pay roadies cash and not make the deductions. Using this method, the roadies or other casual help don't declare their income and don't pay tax on it. While you may be able to save somewhat on the salaries and wages if you do it this way, you will not be able to deduct these cash payments as expenses of the band, and you will pay higher taxes. It is best to make the deductions and complete the proper forms.

e. CONCLUSION

Keeping books for the band can be nerve-racking, tiring, and boring. If you can find a bookkeeper who will do it for a small payment, you're probably best off to let that person handle it. This does not relieve you of the need to keep band records and books of account in a safe place. Nor does it relieve you of the obligation to collect all receipts and identify them as expenses. It will, however, probably save a lot of hassle if you have some qualified bookkeeper to look after your books for you.

If you want to do it on your own, there are certain shortcuts you can take. For example, there are a number of "one-write" accounting systems which get away from double and sometimes triple entry of the financial data. If you are on your own and have no friends or relatives who can assist in the bookkeeping function, this may be a wise route to follow. Check it out with your accountant who will refer you to the available types of one-write systems.

7
RENT, LEASE, OR BUY

It must have been easy being a musician several years ago. All you needed was your guitar and your talent. The guitar could be bought for as little as $5. Add the talent, and you were in business.

Things have changed quite a bit. Who could have foreseen the mountains of equipment needed by a present day rock band? The growth of special effects units, amplifiers, P.A. systems, and lights over the past 15 years has been nothing short of phenomenal. Compare the equipment of today's road band with its P.A. system, mixing disc, monitors, speakers, and amplifiers, to *The Beatles'* electronics of 1964. They played at Shea Stadium using only 50 watts for McCartney's bass and 30 watts each for Harrison and Lennon on guitar. Ringo's drums were unamplified. Today, even a band playing at your local high school would have more power.

Instruments and other equipment have become more expensive over the last few years. Some argue that this means better quality. Others simply point to inflation as the sole cause. For whatever reason, a guitar that cost $200 in 1956 would now probably cost $1,000 or more. Adding special items to it increases the price. It is certainly not unusual for a local band to have $20,000 or more tied up in equipment.

Musicians now require more in the line of instrumentation. Take a look at Ringo's drum set from 1964. Compare that with a double set that is now in use (no doubt due, in large measure, to the influence of Keith Moon). Other percussion instruments have been added, particularly after *Santana's* exploitation of the Latin American sound in the late 1960s.

Instruments used routinely now weren't even made when *The Beatles* started to play. The first electronic synthesizer was not developed until 1964. The original Moog has now expanded to a full range of different keyboards with at least two being used by most bands, thanks to *The Band.*

Even solo performers need a mound of electronic equipment. When was the last time you saw a person with a simple acoustic guitar playing in a lounge? Amplification, sequencers, synthesizers, and other electronic gear unknown 20 years ago are now routine parts of a solo or duo act.

The questions for your band to think about are how much equipment do you acquire, and how do you acquire it?

a. THE INSTRUMENTS

Chances are each member of your group owns his or her own instruments. Because of the personal nature of musical instruments and the desire of most musicians to customize or modify their instruments, they become like old friends, and a rented instrument is just not good enough.

There is little sense in transferring ownership of these items to the band, whether or not the band is incorporated, as these are personal items and members of a group tend to change from time to time, taking their instruments with them.

If each group member owns his or her own instrument, you will also avoid a lot of unpleasant discussions when someone decides to leave. Breaking up is difficult enough. Why add to the problems by arguing over the ownership of equipment?

There is another reason for ownership as opposed to rental or leasing. Generally, an instrument has a long lifetime (unless you believe in breaking it apart at the end of each performance). Many of the top musicians today use instruments that were made over 20 years ago. The technology involved in most instruments is either limited or can be upgraded within the instrument itself, and that technology (unlike amplifiers, P.A. systems, and the other miscellaneous electronic hardware) is not changing too rapidly. This long-term use of the instruments makes buying a better solution.

Each member of the band would normally have a private responsibility to acquire his or her own instruments. The easiest way to do this is by a straight purchase. You pay your money, take the guitar in hand, and go to it. It is best to deal with a reputable retailer or directly with the manufacturer. Because of their portability and value, there are many electric guitars reported stolen every year. That Les Paul you bought from a fellow who was down on his luck may be very nice, but it may also be "hot." If its origin is in doubt, don't buy it. You don't want to end up with the police seizing the instrument and asking you a lot of embarrassing questions at a later date. Better safe than sorry.

b. EQUIPMENT

After the purchase of instruments, you'll have to consider what other equipment you need, and whether or not to buy, lease, or rent.

1. Renting

Renting is temporary. Where the use of the equipment will not be prolonged, renting is probably the best solution. For example, if you normally play small club engagements and have a one-night stand in a large auditorium, rent the equipment, don't buy it or lease it. You pay your money up front, take the equipment for a short period of time and return it to the equipment dealer. Everybody's happy and you don't have to shell out any more money for a temporary piece of equipment.

However, as the band grows, renting may be too expensive and less convenient.

2. Leasing

Leasing equipment is a long-term arrangement. The equipment is owned by your supplier; you agree to use it and to pay for it for a substantial period of time — normally one to two years. During this period, you pay a monthly lease fee. At the end of the term, the equipment is returned to the supplier, who still owns it.

The advantage to this system is that you do not tie up your money in a lot of equipment, nor do you have a big down payment. Most lease arrangements simply call for the first and last months' lease payments to be made at the start. From then on, it is simply a monthly affair. Unfortunately, having made all the payments, you don't own anything. The lease company still owns the equipment.

3. Lease-to-own

Between leasing and owning is an intermediate stage called lease-to-own. This involves a standard lease arrangement with an additional "kicker." At the end of the term and for a predetermined price, you can simply buy the equipment. You don't have to; you can still elect to return it. But if you decide to buy, the end buy out price is quite small because you have been making monthly payments over a long period of time.

This type of lease can be very sophisticated. The monthly payments can be adjusted by extending or compressing time or increasing or decreasing the end purchase price. Most suppliers are quite flexible in this regard. If the type of equipment being acquired is subject to quick technological changes, another advantage is that you don't have to buy the equipment if it becomes obsolete. Nor do you have to try to sell it.

Check with your accountant before you make the decision as to whether equipment should be bought, leased, or leased-to-own. The monthly payments between a loan and a lease may not differ too much. Each, by the way, has its own peculiar tax consequences. Once again, this is something to discuss with your accountant.

4. Buying

Unless one member of the band personally owns a large amount of electronic equipment, it is best for any equipment you plan to purchase to be acquired by the band, instead of by the individual members. First, the band has more buying power. Second, the equipment will be used even if the players in the band change. The musician leaving the band would be removed from any liability in any loan or lease agreement; his or her place would be taken by the new member. If the equipment is purchased by the band as a limited company and no personal guarantee is signed, members of the band are protected from zealous action by the band's creditor if late payments occur.

Your accountant will be delighted with equipment acquisitions. This opens up the world of depreciation, capital costs, and other goodies for tax calculations. Keep your accountant informed about purchases, but let him or her worry about these accounting details.

New equipment acquisitions should be carefully monitored by all members of the band, particularly during the early stages. Sometimes there is a tendency to go absolutely wild in acquiring new equipment. The theory goes, as long as the money is there, the band might as well spend it on new equipment.

In the initial stages of a band's development, most of the band's profits will be plowed back into equipment purchases. Because this is a major expense for any band, each equipment purchase should be carefully examined. Do you really need it? Is it going to be used for a long period of time? Should you lease or buy? If for a limited engagement, wouldn't you be better off renting?

Once your band has made all these decisions and acquired a mountain of equipment, other problems have to be resolved on a day-to-day basis. For example, the equipment has to be stored when not in use. If each band member lives in a small apartment, this could be a problem. You may want to look into a small warehouse where the equipment can be kept out of the wind, weather, and eye of predators. You'll need to carefully compare costs.

c. FINANCING

Paying cash for an instrument or equipment is, without doubt, the cheapest route. No interest accumulates and you are in a better position to bargain.

If you need a loan, check around for rates. A number of people in the money business will be delighted to lend you money to acquire the instrument, and the rates of interest may differ considerably. Although it is convenient to finance through your instrument retailer, check the rate. You may be able to get the money at a better rate down the street at your neighborhood bank. Make sure that you "buy" your money at the best rate possible!

When applying for a loan on an instrument, the lender will want to know a lot about you including your income, past credit history, the cost of the instrument, and the time over which you intend to pay for it. The shorter the time, the less interest paid, and the higher the payments. For example, if you buy a guitar for $1,200 (ignoring interest) and pay for it over one year, the equal monthly payments would be $100. Over two years, the payments would be $50 per month. But when you extend the time of repayment, you increase the interest cost, as your loan is outstanding for a longer period of time.

If the lender is satisfied you are a good credit risk, you may be financed on the basis of what is called a demand loan. This means that there is no actual security. Rather, you sign a promissory note (basically, just a promise to pay the money) and agree to make certain payments. If you fail to make the payments, the lender can sue you on the note and recover from any asset in your possession. A creditor can seize just about everything — not just the instrument.

If security is required, such security is normally represented by the instrument itself. When you are financing through the retailer, this may take the form of a conditional sales agreement. Under this form of purchase, the retailer remains the owner of the instrument until such time as you have completed all payments. When the last payment is made, ownership of the instrument transfers to you. In the interval, if you fail to make any of the payments required, the real owner of the instrument can take it back.

If the lender is not the retailer of the instrument (like a bank or finance company), chances are the loan will be secured by a chattel mortgage. This is like the mortgage of a house. You own it, and can use it, but your ownership is subject to a financial charge in favor of the lender. Once again, if you fail to pay, the lender can seize the instrument.

Where a loan is secured on the instrument, most jurisdictions have special rules that lenders must follow. In many areas, if you default or fail to pay under the loan agreement, the lender can do one of two things. The creditor can seize the instrument or sue you for the balance remaining under the loan agreement. In some areas, the lender can do both. Where this is possible, the lender can seize the instrument, sell it for whatever he or she can get for it, and sue you for the balance that remains. Check with your lawyer to determine the laws in your area.

When you obtain a demand loan for the instrument, the lender is entitled to recover against *any* of your assets. This is because the loan is not specifically secured against the instrument itself; it is secured by your good name and total financial circumstances. This means your car or other personal belongings could be seized as well.

d. OTHER GADGETS

The amount of additional electronic hardware your band will require will depend on the type of music played. A country and western band tends to use less electronic gadgetry than a heavy metal band. A band that normally plays in clubs with its own P.A. system will obviously not need a heavy sound system; a band that limits its engagements to small clubs can also limit its purchase of electronic hardware.

Don't buy anything until you are sure you need it and can afford it.

e. MAKING MONEY FROM YOUR EQUIPMENT

You can, as well, make money from your equipment. As you will be better organized than some of your competitors (and possibly better sounding as well) your equipment, when not in use, can be rented out to others.

Let's say you have a one-week engagement at a club that has its own P.A. system. You could leave your P.A. system in storage where it will simply gather dust. On the other hand, you could rent it out to another band that doesn't have a good P.A. system. The same applies to lights and other individual pieces of electronic hardware.

If you decide on this route, ask your lawyer to prepare a rental agreement that protects you in the event the equipment is misused or abused. When you are not using the equipment, it might as well be making a dollar for you.

8

INSURANCE

When times are tight, it is very easy to overlook insurance payments simply because of the cost. Unfortunately, this can have disastrous effects. There are many different types of insurance you can consider purchasing. You may not need them all, but you should know what's available, and give it some thought.

a. EQUIPMENT INSURANCE

Twenty-five years ago, few, if any, bands would have dreamed of insuring their equipment. The instruments were owned by the individual musicians and, after all, it didn't cost that much to replace a guitar, or a trumpet, or a saxophone. True, the new instrument might not be as good as the old one, but it could be played and an income could be made with it.

With the advent of electronics in the 1950s and the subsequent development of amplifiers, P.A. systems, light shows and other electronic goodies, the cost of fully equipping a band has increased substantially. Individual members of the band still own their personal instruments. However, the mammoth electronics (sound and lights) are normally rented, leased or owned by the band as a unit. If this equipment is stolen or damaged or destroyed in an accident, not only can the band not play, the individual members of the band may be up to their necks in debt trying to pay for equipment that they no longer have.

This risk must be covered by insurance.

Because some of the items to be insured are owned by different people, you need to itemize your inventory of band equipment by owner. Write in the full name of each member of the band who owns equipment, their addresses, and telephone numbers. If the equipment has been bought by the band, indicate this on your form. If any money is owed on the equipment (e.g., a loan from the bank or the equipment supplier), add the name of the creditor to the list with an address. If the equipment is leased or rented, indicate this on your form and provide the name and address of the equipment supplier. Keep this list up-to-date.

Before you contact an insurance agent, take a copy of your list and work out some values. For each item, try to determine when the equipment was acquired and at what cost. Next (and perhaps after talking with a music instrument dealer or equipment supplier), find out how much it would cost to replace it with new equipment — assuming everything was lost tomorrow. This is called replacement cost. Because the price of everything tends to go up, the replacement cost may well be substantially higher than the cost of equipment when initially bought.

With this information in hand, you are now ready to shop for your insurance. What you are after is called a general insurance agent. This is a person who arranges insurance on things and not people.

Try to get a policy that covers all of the equipment and its replacement cost or full value. This may be difficult to get for two reasons. First, because the equipment is owned by different parties it is a more difficult procedure. This is why you have prepared your list with the name and addresses of the owners. It makes the task of the insurance agent a little easier.

The second reason for difficulty is the aspect of replacement cost. Let's use an example. Your lead guitarist has a classic 1950s two-tone maple neck sunburst solid Fender Stratocaster in excellent condition. He picked it up in a remote secondhand shop four years ago for $100. That price is his cost. The value of the guitar to a collector or a musician is quite high — approximately $2,000. If the guitar was lost or stolen, your guitarist would have to pay his replacement cost to get a guitar equal to the lost item. Make sense? Sure it does, but you may have difficulty convincing the insurance companies of that.

To an insurance company, the guitar is worth its original cost, less depreciation, for a value they call depreciated value. In this case, the insurance company would take the original cost, subtract four years worth of depreciation (after all, it is a "used guitar") and pay out the figure obtained. Probably, the depreciated value of the guitar, when viewed in this fashion, would be no more than $50. Now, there is a big difference between $50 and $2,000. This is why you want replacement cost insurance on the items the band owns, leases or rents. If you don't have it, all you get is the $50. If you do, you collect the full cost of replacing the Stratocaster with an identical Stratocaster (or one of equal value), and not simply another used guitar.

The same approach can be followed with all the equipment the band uses. To get a good idea of what the replacement cost is, talk to equipment dealers and instrument retailers. After all, these are the people from whom you will have to buy the replacement items.

Another matter to consider is that equipment changes over time. Your 1960 amplifier might do quite well but it may not be made any more. You will want insurance that will replace the amplifier with a new amplifier that does the job as well or better. Talk all of these items over with your insurance agent and make sure it is clear who owns what and what you want to insure and for how much. Confirm any understanding by letter. Read the policy when it is delivered and make sure all members of the band understand what is insured and for how much. Review it annually, or after large purchases, and be sure to keep your insurance agent and your policy up-to-date whenever you add or change equipment.

Ideally, you would insure your equipment for what is called all perils. This means that even if the equipment is simply misplaced by you, it will be replaced. This is an extremely expensive type of insurance. Once again, discuss this with your insurance agent.

Try to make sure that your insurance agent understands what it is the band does. If necessary, give your insurance agent this book to read over the weekend. Most insurance agents have little comprehension of the business side of music and will be astounded at the actual cost of the equipment you use. Be prepared to take some time to get the coverage you want.

If you have problems finding an agent who will deal with musicians, you might have to state your occupation as business person. Try to find a friendly insurance agent and check things over with him or her before you fill out your occupation on the application forms.

Insurance for band equipment is expensive. If you are going to pay the shot, make sure the insurance will cover you for the anticipated losses. In addition to your list of equipment, save all purchase receipts to verify the value in the case of loss. It also may help to engrave your social security number or other coded symbol on your pieces of equipment. If anything is stolen, this identification can help you to get it back.

b. AUTO INSURANCE

Another necessary item of equipment for most bands is its vehicle, which is often a van. The van is not usually owned by the band itself — rather it is owned by one member who makes it available for the band's use. Or, perhaps members of the band travel to an engagement on their own in their own vehicles.

Most auto insurance companies have different rates for business use and for pleasure driving. The rate is higher if the vehicle is used for commercial or business purposes. Driving to and from work is viewed by most insurance companies as an additional use. If you use the van or your own vehicles to get to and from engagements on a regular basis, chances are you now qualify for the additional premium.

You don't *have* to tell your auto insurance agent about this. But if you don't, and you have an accident, you may find that your coverage is reduced or non-existent.

Check this aspect with your auto insurance agent. Explain what the vehicle is used for and specify (in writing if necessary) how many times it is used to go to and from an engagement. If you are advised that this is not viewed as a commercial use, get it in writing. Ask the agent for a letter clarifying what you have been told so that you can show it to the other members of the band. Keep this letter with your insurance policy in a safe place. That way, if you are subsequently denied coverage because of the purported commercial use of the van, you have the agent's own representations to fall back on.

c. LIABILITY INSURANCE

Twenty years ago, there wasn't much damage you could do to another person with a musical instrument. True, a person could trip over a guitar, fall, and break a leg. But the chances of this happening were remote given the nature of entertainment as it was then. The chances of severe injury to another person were equally remote.

This has now changed considerably. Members of the audience are encouraged to get close to the band even if a stage platform is used. The band itself uses instruments that have a high electrical output and this electricity represents a danger. Your P.A. system may be controlled from a remote location in which case cords, wires and gear generally lead through the dance area. All of this points to potential liability if someone gets hurt and increases the possibility of a major injury.

With this in mind, you should check with your insurance agent about liability insurance. If an over-enthusiastic fan sticks his or her finger in your amplifier (even if the fan wasn't supposed to be anywhere near the amplifier), you may be found liable to pay for the fan's injuries. With the growing cost of medical expenses, this could be quite high. Cover yourself. Liability insurance of this type is relatively inexpensive and should be obtained for a high value.

Remember, you are not an employee of the clubs that hire you; you are an independent contractor. An injured patron might sue the band as well as the club. If the band is not incorporated, this means suing each and every member of the band personally. This means that your own car, motorcycle and, yes, your 1955 Stratocaster is up for grabs if you are found liable and cannot meet the payments. A little insurance in this area goes a long way if an injury occurs.

d. INSURING THE BAND MEMBERS

Thus far, we have been looking at insuring things or other people. Now we have to look at insuring the band members themselves.

Most bands don't bother with this. Whether this is a wise decision depends on whether or not a problem arises. Once again, you have to balance the cost of the insurance against the potential risk. That calls for another meeting of the band.

1. Life insurance

First, there is life insurance. Think about the equipment the band bought two months ago. Would you be able to find a replacement for a missing musician quickly enough to keep the payments going? What if the missing musician is also your lead singer and best known member? Things might get a little rough. It is possible to obtain low cost term life insurance to cover this potential risk.

Look at your equipment list once again. How much is financed? What do you owe? You should insure each member of the band for this amount. If any member is killed the insurance on the life would then pay the balance owed for the equipment. This would give you at least some time to replace the missing member without the worry of the monthly loan payments. As the members of your group are probably quite young, in good health, and not in a hazardous occupation, the cost of this insurance would be quite small.

As the reputation of the band increases, the need for such insurance rises as well. At a particular stage, you will want to consider key-person insurance. Could you imagine

The Rolling Stones without Mick Jagger? Pretty difficult, isn't it. What if Mick were killed in an auto accident tomorrow — could the band go on? If it did, would its income be the same? Probably not.

Members of a band can protect themselves from this type of loss by insuring the life of their lead singer. If something happens, they receive the insurance as a form of compensation for the loss of income. Obviously, you don't have to worry about this aspect until you've hit the big time.

For this type of insurance, you need a life insurance agent. There are lots of these around. Find one you can talk with and discuss the issue with him or her.

You may have to pay out a spouse or family of a deceased member of the band for that portion of interest in the business. If this is the case, life insurance is mandatory. Let's say the band is "worth" $10,000 at the time a member dies. What does the family get as its share of the "asset" at the time of death? Although this gets rather complicated, it is something to review with your lawyer and your life insurance agent on a regular basis, particularly if the band has developed a solid reputation and is going places. After all, even the name may have a substantial value if things go well. There are, sorry to say, tax consequences to this issue as well. You may want to involve your accountant if you think it necessary.

You can also check with your local union to determine if they offer group insurance, which may be much cheaper. The New York local of the A.F. of M. offers a group plan, for example, as do other locals.

2. Disability insurance

Another type of insurance for band members to consider is disability insurance. If a band member suffers an injury that makes it impossible to work, this insurance will provide a monthly income. The amount of the monthly income, the length of waiting time, the length of time it will continue, as well as the member's age, health and other factors, all affect the premium. Once again, there are certain tax considerations.

If the members of the band have other occupations to fall back on, this probably isn't too relevant. For a full-time musician, however, it is.

As with people in other businesses, band members should be conscious of potential health risks in their occupation. They are exposed to certain health hazards including electrical wiring and excessive sound levels. If the individual members of the band think it important enough, they should review disability insurance with their life insurance agent. At least find out the cost of this disability insurance before you run into a problem, and make a rational decision. Check into it and determine whether or not you need it, and if you can, or should, pay for it.

e. HEALTH AND TRAVEL INSURANCE

Something often overlooked by musicians is basic health insurance. You may be healthy as a horse today but tomorrow may be a bit different. All members of the band should be covered for their basic medical insurance. In Canada, this is relatively easy as such insurance is available through your provincial government at a small cost. In the United States, it becomes a bit more difficult but even so, the premiums are relatively low.

A musician who goes out on the road without this basic coverage is asking for trouble. In the event of injury, not only does it take him or her off work and eliminate income, but it also creates a hefty bill for medical costs.

If you are travelling over state or provincial borders or, indeed, over the Canada-U.S. border, make sure you have insurance coverage in place that will cover you in the other state or province. If, for example, a Canadian musician from Vancouver plays an engagement in Seattle and is injured in Seattle, his Canadian health insurance may not cover all of his U.S. medical expenses. Consider purchasing additional insurance prior to departing for an international engagement.

70

f. CONCLUSION

As with any other business, a band could literally spend all of its receipts solely on insurance. You have to make some hard decisions. What risks do you really *have* to cover? What risks do you want to cover? As part of your regular band business meetings, you should review insurance from time to time. Make sure you understand the policies that you obtain and ask questions where you don't.

9

UNIONS — TO JOIN OR NOT TO JOIN

Chances are you know at least one person who is a member of a union. In most industries, the function of the union is fairly obvious and direct. If you work at Enormous Manufacturing Co. Ltd. on its assembly line, you know that all of the workers are members of the same union. You also know that if you don't belong to the union, generally, you don't get to work. (There are exceptions in certain "right-to-work states in the U.S.).

In manufacturing or other similar industries, the presence and function of the union is readily apparent. Not so with the music business.

The unions involved in the music business act for a number of "independent contractors." Their members are scattered around the countryside playing in different clubs, taverns, and pubs. Some are employed only for a day, others for a week, others for longer. This is substantially more complicated than the normal type of union involvement.

To make things worse, a number of places that use live music are non-union. A number of bands are non-union, particularly new groups or those that are midway between amateur and professional status. In many areas, the majority of clubs are non-union. Some amateurs will work for nothing just for the experience. Some members of the union (even though they are not supposed to) will, under their own or an assumed name, work in non-union establishments.

In the music business, particularly in your early stages, the choice between union principles and a job is a difficult one to make — perhaps your most difficult in the early stages of your career.

72

Whether or not you should immediately join the union after you have started your career as a professional musician is, like other matters, one of personal choice. Staunch union members would say that you should join the minute you start to avoid being financially hurt. Others, recognizing that there are other considerations, suggest that you not join the union until your career has advanced to the point where you are playing in larger clubs (which tend to be union), or you are playing with other union members and look to them for additional work, or your agent is licensed by the union and can get you enough work to keep going.

Before you make the decision to join or not to join, look around, ask what others are doing and, in particular, try to find out how many establishments in your area are union or non-union. If the majority, if not all, are union, your choice is pretty well made. If most of the places you expect to be playing during the early stages of your career are non-union much of your decision is also made (bear in mind that the union requirement is to play only at union shops.) Look around in your local area before you take the plunge.

Some musicians try to combine the best of both worlds. They join the union under their own name and work on a day-to-day basis under another non-union name in non-union clubs. For a time, they might be able to get away with this. But, eventually, something has to give. This route is *not* recommended. Make a conscious decision as to which route you are going, and stick to it.

In the early stages of your career, there is a choice. Sometimes the choice is dictated by the area in which you are attemtping to establish yourself. However, there is little doubt that as you progress up the ladder in the music business you will have to join the union. Quite simply, the more your stature increases, the more you will want to play larger engagements and, more frequently than not, these will be union engagements.

a. THE UNIONS IN THE MUSIC BUSINESS

The largest union in the music business is the American Federation of Musicians of the United States and Canada, known as A.F. of M. This union has been around since the late 1800s and acts on behalf of professional musicians. It has over 600 locals and a membership of over 300,000. On behalf of its member professional musicians, it attempts to regulate wages and working conditions on the international, national, and local levels. International and national matters are normally handled through offices in New York (for the United States) or Toronto (for Canada). The addresses for the two headquarters are found in the Appendix. Naturally enough, local wage rates and conditions are handled by the local of your area, subject to certain controls from higher up.

The A.F. of M. acts for "professional musicians," which may cause a problem with your vocalist. Your singer may not be qualified to join this union, (depending on the rules of the local in your area). Important as your lead singer is, he or she may have to qualify (once again depending upon local rules) for a membership as a tambourine player, or something similar. This is because jurisdiction of the A.F. of M. is limited to professional musicians, and as vocalists are not classed as professional musicians by most locals, jurisdiction is split. This does not mean that your vocalist cannot be a member of a union. He or she may, however, have to look to another union for representation.

If so, this union will be the American Guild of Variety Artists, otherwise known as AGVA. This union acts for vocalists in live entertainment as well as other types of non-musical acts, such as magicians and comedians.

Before your vocalist joins A.F. of M. or AGVA, he or she should carefully consider the merits of both unions. Check with the local of A.F. of M. in your area to determine the rules. If your vocalist has a choice, he or she should talk to other vocalists to determine which union they have joined and why.

Generally, these two unions cover all unionized performers of live music. However, other affiliations may be necessary as your band gains stature or as you take on additional jobs aside from playing solely for the band.

The American Guild of Music Artists (AGMA) is quite "high brow." Its members are generally involved in classical music.

Singing for radio and television puts you into the realm of the American Federation of Television and Radio Artists, or AFTRA. Studio work by singers is also covered by this group.

In Canada, the same area is occupied by the Alliance of Canadian Cinema, Television and Radio Artists, or ACTRA, which also in some instances covers studio musicians.

Looking further afield (and, generally, only after you have been a member of one of the preceding unions for at least one year) and depending upon the actual engagement for film or commercial, you may have to consider the Screen Actors' Guild Inc., or SAG.

It's certainly possible to be a member of more than one union as the fields covered by the various unions tend to overlap. For example, if you are also a songwriter, you would normally be a member of a performing rights organization and, perhaps, the Songwriters' Guild (which is an association, not a union).

b. WHAT DOES THE UNION DO?

Like any union, the music business unions try to regulate working conditions and wages for their members. However, they have more than their share of problems. This is because of the number of separate employers who employ their membership. Also, because membership in the union is not mandatory within the industry — for either the employers or the employees — there is more than the normal amount of tension and turmoil.

Even if you don't join the union, you should be familiar with the minimum standards established by it for engagements. This will at least tell you if you are being paid more or less than the standard.

Let's assume you have decided to join the A.F. of M., or AGVA. What can you expect?

The union local in your area will provide minimum pay standards for any engagement. Established on a local basis, these pay scales cover one-night stands as well as longer engagements, and represent minimum standards. As a member of the union, you can negotiate a fee greater than the minimum but are not permitted to work for anything under the minimum. Simple as it sounds, this presents a number of problems because of the particular nature of the music business.

For example, some musicians work under assumed names when they have a non-union gig. It is not unknown for a bar or tavern to enter into two contracts with the entertainers — one at the required level of wages (called "at scale") and the other at a lesser amount. Needless to say, the lesser amount is the one actually paid. In other instances, the club will deduct a fee for promotion and advertising from the amount paid to your band. There are a number of methods used by clubs and sometimes even by musicians to avoid union requirements. For the employers, these "deals" represent a savings; for the musician, such a deal may represent work when otherwise there may not be any.

The local union also establishes certain minimum standards concerning working conditions. The length of sets and breaks between sets are established. Depending upon the local, some attempt is made to police these and other conditions of employment. This is done by the business representative of the union for your area. To check out what these conditions are, contact the local of A.F. of M. or AGVA in your area and obtain a copy of their current agreement. Even though the language may be difficult, read it over and get your lawyer to interpret what you don't understand.

The A.F. of M. is attempting to establish additional health standards to protect its members. There are certain health hazards apparent in many clubs — the noise level being the worst offender.

The unions have also established other norms. For example, the union band must have a written contract with its employers. This is a good idea whether you are unionized or not as it protects both parties.

The union also licences booking agents. A licenced booking agent is only permitted to book union acts in union clubs. Once again, the standard union agreement protects both parties.

A.F. of M. has established a music performance trust fund which requires an additional payment by your employer. This additional payment is generally used for the union to sponsor performances of their members on a charitable basis, at least for the audience. Generally all union members who play in such performances are paid at least scale. And, as with other unions, many of the locals have established a pension fund. Check to determine whether or not your local has done so. Don't underestimate this benefit. You're young and strong now, but you might not be so in the future. Other locals have established special clauses covering life and disability insurance, equipment insurance, and so on. Once again, check with the local in your area to determine if they can be of assistance to you. These incentives for membership can be quite beneficial.

Not to be forgotten is the union "black book" or "black list." Because of the nature of the business, the A.F. of M. tries to keep track of those employers that are not quite up to snuff. This list is simply a list of those clubs, taverns, and other similar places that use non-union entertainment. The "defaulters' list" is perhaps more relevant. It lists names of establishments that have welshed on the deal. When an employer has not paid entertainers, his or her name will be included on this list.

c. BASICS OF MEMBERSHIP

Except for those states that have right-to-work legislation, a member of either of the performing unions is not permitted to work on a non-union engagement or with non-union entertainers. This can result in suspension, fines, or other penalties being imposed by your local. Check out all of the union regulations after reading them through with your lawyer. Only after you have done this should you make your decision to join or not to join.

Don't forget that the union costs you money. As with any union, there are the costs of joining (called initiation fees), annual dues, and the like, all of which must be paid. In some cases, your agent or manager will do this for you. If you receive payment from your engagements directly, you are responsible for remitting the amounts due to the union. You will probably be penalized by the union if you fail to remit the amounts due.

If you decide to join, make it worthwhile. Many unions seem to function only through the apathy of their members. A small group — perhaps those who do not have many engagements — can obtain control of the local. They may establish local conditions which are unacceptable to you or simply impossible for you to follow. If you have joined the union, make sure that you try to attend union meetings. In particular, review all new rules that attempt to establish certain industry standards. Having joined the union, you don't want it to amend its policies to make your type of work impossible. Keep your address up-to-date with the union so they know how to contact you.

Sample #1 shows the application for membership in the American Federation of Musicians.

If you join, participate. Only if you do so can the union function effectively. A well-functioning local can be a benefit not only to its members but also to the music business generally. A mismanaged local can have disastrous consequences for its members and the performance of live music generally. In Canada, for example, AGVA has been relatively ineffective. Fortunately, the A.F. of M. has managed to fill the void that otherwise would exist. Check with musicians locally and understand as much of the union activities as you can before you make a commitment to join.

SAMPLE #1
UNION MEMBERSHIP APPLICATION

American Federation of Musicians
of the United States and Canada

APPLICATION BLANK

FOR USE IN CANADA ONLY

Local No. 145

I, the undersigned, make application to become a member of Local   145   of the American Federation of Musicians of the United States and Canada. If my application is accepted, I do hereby promise and agree that I will faithfully and at all times conform to, and be bound by, the Constitution, By-Laws, Rules, Regulations, Resolutions and Tariff of Fees of said Local, and the American Federation of Musicians of the United States and Canada, as they now exist, and as they may be altered, amended, or repealed at any time in the future while I am a member. I declare that the answers herein given are complete and true to the best of my knowledge and belief, and in the event that it shall be proven that I have answered untruthfully, I agree to forfeit all fees paid to the Local of the American Federation of Musicians of the United States and Canada, as the case may be.

1. Name _____ Alice Morrison _____

(Professional Name) _____

Social Insurance Number _____ 803 445 617 _____

Present Address _____ 1566 _____ South Main Street _____

(Street No.   Street Name   Apt. No.)

City _____ Vancouver _____ Postal Code _____ V8T 1Y7 _____

Telephone Number _____ 869-2245 _____

Date of Birth _____ May 10, 1957 _____

What instrument(s) do you play? _____ Keyboard; piano _____

_____

_____ Vocals? YES _X_ NO _____

2. How long have you resided in this jurisdiction? _____ since 1979 _____

3. Are you a member of any branch of the Armed Forces? _____ No _____

4. Are you at present a member of any Local of the American Federation of Musicians in Canada or the United States?
YES _____ NO _X_

If yes name Local _____

5. Have you ever been suspended, erased, or expelled from any Local of the American Federation of Musicians in Canada or the United States? YES _____ NO _X_

If yes, when and where? _____

For what cause? _____

6. Have you been imported into this country by an agent, musical director, employer, or any other person?
YES _____ NO _X_

7. Recommended by _____ Tommy Jo Raymond _____

8. Signature of applicant _____ *Alice Morrison* _____

Date _____ November 13 _____ 19 _8-_

BOND

The undersigned does hereby pledge himself as Surety for _____ a minor, until he has reached his majority, who promises to faithfully support the Constitution, By-Laws and Tariff of Fees of the _____ and the provisions as enumerated in the above application. and that in case of any violation of the same, the undersigned will be responsible for all such charges brought, or fines imposed against said person.

Witnessed by _____ Signed _____ Surety.

FOR OFFICE USE ONLY

This application was made on _____ 19 _____

Signed by _____
Secretary of Local No. 145

Indoctrination Program viewed on _____ 19 _____

30

10

ENGAGEMENT CONTRACTS

a. THE BASICS

If you are a member of a union, your union business representative will prescribe forms of engagement contracts for use by you, your booking agent, and a union club. One requirement of unions is that any engagement be subject to a written agreement. If you are travelling to the United States or Canada, you will have to provide a copy of your written agreement as evidence of your employment when crossing the border.

In these two instances, a contract between your band and an employer must be in writing. In all other cases, a written contract isn't essential, but for your own protection, you should have one. A good written contract can mean the difference between success and failure in the music business.

The purpose of getting everything down in writing is to avoid confusion at a later time about what was agreed, and to protect both parties. For example, you want to be protected from an employer who claims not to have agreed to provide accommodations or meals, and can't remember whether the engagement was to be three or four days. You want to tie down all the details.

On the other hand, be sure that you will show up on time each night of your engagement. The contract must serve both sides.

The contract between any band and its employer is different from many contracts prepared by lawyers. As your business is music, the contract involves artistic considerations. It is a personal service contract and, as such, special rules apply. Also, you are not an employee; you are an independent contractor and, therefore, more in need of a contract tailored to your individual requirements.

b. CHARACTERISTICS OF A PERSONAL SERVICE CONTRACT

Being in a band involves playing music. Music is a form of art. Contracts that deal with art are somewhat different from the normal contracts that deal solely with the exchange of goods for money. Because personal taste is involved, these contracts normally have an element of discretion not found in other contracts. In order to live up to the terms of any contract, your standard of performance cannot vary. If it does, the variation might be sufficient to justify termination of an engagement on aesthetic grounds.

For example, let's assume you are a Top 40 group. An employer receives your promo kit, likes the demo tape, and you pass the test at the audition. You and the employer enter into a contract for a future engagement. Between the audition and your appearance at the club, your band changes its emphasis. You decide to move to New Wave music. Now, the members of your band are still the same, but the music has changed substantially. Is your initial contract with this employer valid? Chances are it isn't. At least, not unless you go back to playing Top 40.

If your employer has an established type of music in the club, and you have changed your music from that standard, the employer doesn't have to keep the contract. If you do substantially change your routine, make sure you tell all parties with whom you have entered into a contract. If they agree to the change — fine. If not, you'd better look for a new engagement.

In other cases, your employer can terminate an engagement if you are not performing up to standard, for example, if some members of the band are half intoxicated by the second set and your music suffers, or if you are just having a series of bad nights and can't "get it together." After all, you are hired as professional musicians who can play up to standard every night. Your employer can get amateurs who don't play to a consistent standard any-where — and for a much smaller price. Both for your own satisfaction and for your employer's happiness, you have to play up to standard each and every night.

If your band takes on new personnel after the audition and before the engagement because your lead singer, lead guitar, and keyboard all quit, your contract may not be binding.

A personal service contract is rather peculiar. An employer hires a specific band because of its unique and particular characteristics. If the characteristics change you may have problems.

If you do have a substantial change in the personnel of your band, let your future employers know and give them the opportunity for another audition *before* you run into problems.

Another attribute of a personal service contract is that it cannot be enforced by what lawyers call "specific perfor-mance." If you break the contract and don't perform, your employer cannot go to court and force you to perform. However, you can be sued for damages. The employer can also restrain you from playing in other locations where a contract exists between you and the club.

c. RULES OF THE HOUSE

Every employer has particular house rules concerning entertainers. If legal, can you drink alcohol when perform-ing? Can you drink between sets? Are your drinks on the house up to a maximum limit or do you have to pay for them? If so, at what price? Is there a discount? Are guests permitted when the employer provides accommodation? What about guests at dinner?

These, and other house rules, should be checked with your employer at the time you negotiate your contract.

Ask the employer what particular rules exist — whether written or unwritten. Try to get this information before you agree to an engagement.

d. TERMS OF A CONTRACT

The A.F. of M., AGVA, and other unions have standard form contracts for engagements. Sample #2 shows an engagement contract used by the A.F. of M. Even if you are not a member of these unions, you may want to write to them and obtain a copy of their standard contract forms. They will give you an indication of what should be in your contract.

Items normally included in a contract are discussed below.

1. Payment

Naturally enough, the amount you are to be paid should be specified. Also the terms of the payment should be spelled out. Some bands like to be paid nightly. If you would like this, specify it in the contract. Will you be paid by cash or check? If by check, can it be cashed at the bar after the last set?

2. Number of performances

The number of performances and their duration should be specified. The time of all sets and the time of all breaks should also be included.

3. Type of music

The type of music to be played is not always specified in a contract, but it is a good idea to describe your style, (e.g., Top 40, rhythm & blues, etc.).

4. Accommodation and meals

If accommodation is provided, the terms should be contained in the contract. This applies to meals as well.

SAMPLE #2
A.F. OF M. CONTRACT

FOR USE BY LOCAL 145 MEMBERS WITHIN LOCAL 145 JURISDICTION ONLY

CONTRACT

American Federation of Musicians
of the United States and Canada
Local 145
510-207 WEST HASTINGS ST.
VANCOUVER, B.C. V6B 1J6

CONTRACT No.

F 47921

THIS CONTRACT for the personal services of musicians, made this **5th** day of **March** 19 8–. between the undersigned purchaser (hereinafter called the "purchaser") and **two** musicians (hereinafter called "employees"). WITNESSETH, That the purchaser employs the services of the employees as musicians severally and the employees severally through their representative (leader or contractor) agree to render collectively to the purchaser services as musicians according to the terms and conditions contained herein. The terms and conditions on the reverse side hereof are an express part of this contract as though set out in full below.

TYPE OF ENGAGEMENT (SPECIFY) (PLEASE PRINT) __Nightclub__

SPONSORING ORGANIZATION (PLEASE PRINT) _____

PLACE OF ENGAGEMENT __GoForIt Club__ ADDRESS __1382 Washington Dr., Calgary, Alberta__

LEADER __Henry Fox__ ADDRESS __732 North Ave., Calgary, Alberta__

CASUAL ENGAGEMENTS	CONTINUING ENGAGEMENTS
DATE OF ENGAGEMENT __March 5, 198–__	DATE(S) OF ENGAGEMENT _____
HOURS OF ENGAGEMENT _____	HOURS OF ENGAGEMENT _____
FROM __8:00 P.M.__	NO. OF DAYS PER WEEK _____
TO __12:00 P.M.__	NUMBER OF MUSICIANS (INCLUDING LEADER) _____
DATE OF REHEARSALS __Nil__	WEEKLY FEE AGREED ON $ _____
FROM __N/A__ TO __N/A__	SCHEDULE OF PAYMENTS _____
FEE AGREED ON $ __250.00__	SPECIAL CONDITIONS (OVERTIME, EXPENSES, ETC.)
	N/A

EMPLOYEES (PLEASE PRINT)	MINIMUM BASIC FEE	EXTRA FEES*	TOTAL NEGOTIATED FEES	SOCIAL INSURANCE NO.
Henry Fox LEADER	$ 150.00	$ N/A	$ 150.00	780-521-103
Shirley Fox	75.00	N/A	75.00	730-960-605
TOTAL	**$225.00**		**$225.00**	

GoForIt Club
PURCHASER'S NAME
per: _Rdevana_
SIGNATURE OF PURCHASER
1382 Washington Drive
ADDRESS
Calgary   Alberta
CITY   _PROVINCE_
PHONE

Henry Fox
LEADER'S NAME
Henry Fox
SIGNATURE OF LEADER
732 North Avenue
ADDRESS
Calgary   Alberta
CITY   _PROVINCE_
LEADER'S REPRESENTATIVE

5. Set-up times

Make sure that the time for set-up is agreeable to both parties.

6. Decibel level

Increasingly, because of municipal by-laws and health considerations, employers are concerned about the level of sound. If this has to be specified, do so in the contract and give the employer the final say.

7. Equipment damage

Will the employer cover the cost of repairing your equipment if damaged by a patron? Specify in the contract to avoid arguments later.

8. Options

If there is an option for a further engagement, get it in writing along with the time by which such options may be exercised.

9. Travel allowance

If your employer is going to pay a portion of your travel expenses, get this in writing in the contract.

10. Names of parties to the contract

The contract should, of course, properly identify both the employer and your band. This may sound simple but because of certain variables, there are many possibilities.

For your employer, the name could be any of the following:

(a) Kit Kat Tavern Ltd. — for a company that uses the company name for its business name.

(b) Ventures Tavern Ltd., carrying on business under the firm and style of Kit Kat Tavern — where the company name and trade name differ.

(c) Melvin Highball, carrying on business under the firm name and style of Kit Kat Tavern — where your employer is not incorporated and uses a particular business name.

Your band might be named as:

(a) High Jinx Music Inc. where the band name and its performing name are the same.

(b) West Coast Sound Inc., carrying on business under the band name of The High Jinx — where the company name and band name differ.

(c) Randy Smith, Sandy Jones, William Taylor, Tracy Evans, and Paul Novak, carrying on business under the name The High Jinx — where the band is a partnership using a particular name.

In addition to naming the parties, it is advisable to include the names, addresses, and social insurance or security numbers of all members of the band as a schedule or appendix to the contract. You don't have to do this, but it's a nice touch. If you are crossing the border for an engagement, it's very helpful.

e. PLAYING THE DOOR

"Playing the door" can be a good financial arrangement that some bands prefer. Or, it can be a financial disaster. If you choose this arrangement, put the details in your contract.

Under this arrangement, your employer charges an entry fee or cover charge for the place where you are performing. You band is paid from this cover charge and not from the employer's other receipts (such as the sale of liquor and so on). This type of arrangement can have a number of variations. You could get all of the cover charges (or the "gate") or only a percentage of them. Certainly, your contract should specify how much of the gate you receive.

The contract should also specify how many people, at a maximum, can get in free. If your employer lets a lot of friends in, money will be collected from the drinks sold, but you might not get much at all.

Be cautious before entering into this arrangement. Check out the size of the club and try and find out what its average attendance is. Make sure your contract includes the weekend, not just the slow days during the early part of the week. If possible, chat with other bands who have played at the club under the same arrangement. What was their take?

In this type of arrangement, you might want one of your friends to come along on the gig, to stand by the front door and count the people coming in. The tally should equal that reported by the club owner.

f. WHO PREPARES THE CONTRACT?

The contract can be prepared on your union form or by your employer, your booking agent, or by your band (with advice from your lawyer).

It is very important when you start off that each member of the band sees the contract and understands what it says. Meet with your lawyer to review it or if there is anything in the contract you don't understand or have doubts about. At the very least, have your lawyer review the first one or two contracts you sign so that you understand what they are all about.

For convenience, many groups standardize their own contracts. This applies to employers, booking agents, and bands. It certainly helps if you are able to use a contract for a number of engagements which you fully understand and which does the job. If you prepare a standard form, you can have copies made so all you have to do is fill in the blanks when you get an actual performance.

Your lawyer can prepare a standard engagement contract for your band. Use it whenever you can. That way, you know what is in it and can understand it, and you don't have to review each and every contract with the band. If your lawyer draws up this type of contract for you, it should contain all the elements referred to earlier.

If your booking agent has a standard form, you might consider using this. Before you do, take it to your lawyer to review it. If there is something to be added, do so. Once again, because the contract is intended for routine use, you won't have to review the specific provisions every time you sign.

The employer may, as well, have a standard form contract. If so, read it over before you sign it. If there are differences between this agreement and the agreement that your lawyer or booking agent has prepared, make sure you understand them.

Remember the two rules we referred to earlier for contracts:

(a) Get it in writing, and

(b) Make sure you understand it before you sign it.

Your contract need not be long — one or two pages will be quite sufficient. As long as the basic terms are included, you should not have too many problems. The contract for an engagement should be signed after the audition and before the engagement. After all, if your employer phones to cancel before you have shown up, you want some proof in writing if you have to sue. Remember, as well, if you employ a booking agent or other personal representative that his or her percentage should be included (or at least kept in mind) in the calculation of the engagement fee.

g. CORRECTING MISTAKES

Let us say you went wrong somewhere along the way. You've signed a bad contract with a bad manager. Is all lost?

The answer to that is very simple. It depends on how much somebody else wants you.

Any contract you sign can be revised with the consent of the other party. If you are willing to pay the price, chances are you can get out of a past mistake. Performers have been able to avoid bad management contracts, or bad recording contracts, by negotiating with the other side and arriving at a conclusion satisfactory to both sides. It normally involves a considerable amount of money; but it can avoid, or make tolerable, a problem which has developed from earlier years.

This does not mean to say that the contracts that you enter into are not binding. They are, unless there is some legal technicality which voids the contract, or unless all parties to the contract mutually agree to cancel the contract.

If you have arrived at a major stage in your career — particularly a recording contract — you may wish to review all of your other contracts and the successes or failures of the people with whom you have been involved. The longer you wait, the more difficult it becomes to review these contracts and to arrive at settlement terms for cancellation. Until they are cancelled (and in the absence of any legal reasons for terminating them), those contracts are binding.

11

CROSSING THE LINE

Music is international. A song recorded in West Germany may well find its way to North America. Many North American songs are played worldwide. Musicians travel from place to place for employment and to further their career. Indeed, one of the characteristics of a musical life tends to be living out of a suitcase.

In North America, where the entertainment business of the United States and Canada is so closely intertwined, crossing the border between the two countries is quite normal. A band from the United States will often find an engagement in Canada, and vice versa.

Both the United States and Canada have immigration laws that cover temporary visitors to each country. As visitors, Americans and Canadians enjoy relatively free access to each other's countries. However, as a rule, this visitor status is limited to no more than 90 days and employment is not allowed.

You need government permission to work in another country. Usually, you need a visa and a work permit. Permission to go to the other country and work may be refused, or made subject to certain terms and conditions.

a. GENERAL GUIDELINES

Although the laws of Canada and the United States differ in detail, the general principles are the same. You can only work across the line if you obtain the necessary permit. With the exception of well known musicians with international reputations, you will only be granted a work permit if giving the job to a foreigner will not deprive a native of work opportunities. As well, as a visitor you have to satisfy other standards. A prior criminal record, false statements in your application, or even health problems may be sufficient to refuse the application and deny the permission necessary to work.

There are, in reality, two hurdles to get over. For immigration, the government has to be satisfied about your character; for employment, you have to prove you're not depriving a native of a job opportunity. Pass these two tests and you get in.

If your band earns "world class" status, special rules apply. The employment test is deleted; only the immigration test remains. Status is proven by reference to reviews, engagements, and other indicators. The government may refer this question to the relevant union. It takes some time and substantial success before a band can qualify for world status.

Because you're just starting out, both tests apply. In addition, to prove the offer of employment is valid, a written copy of the contract must be presented to the government. Once the employment test is passed, you will be checked for criminal records and other matters. A final check is made at the border before you are allowed entry.

Both countries have special rules for entertainers. A Canadian does not have to apply in person; an agent may do so or you can apply by mail (normally your employer or booking agent will do this for you). Concerts and other events are treated differently from a gig at a pub or tavern. Last-minute or emergency situations are also afforded special status. A Canadian needed as a last-minute replacement would get speedy treatment, provided the emergency is genuine.

After receiving permission to work in the United States, a Canadian must cross the border at a specified port of entry to make sure all forms are available and ready. Canadians are limited as to where and when they can work in the States; if the engagement is extended, or a new gig added to the tour, they have to apply from within the United States for a modification to the initial work permit. If they overstay the time allowed, or breach any of the conditions imposed, they can be asked, or forced, to leave the country.

In both countries, no attempt will be made to judge your music (other than in extreme cases) and flexibility is maintained. But you should not accept a job in the other country without checking as to who will apply for the necessary permit, or if you have reason to believe that permission will not be granted (for example, if you have been busted in the last year).

b. FLYING NORTH — WORKING IN CANADA

If you get a gig in Canada, you or your employer must apply for employment authorization. Your contract and other particulars are submitted to a Canada Employment Centre for approval. If the permit is granted, you will receive a Form 2151 which sets out the conditions under which you may work in Canada.

Television and radio engagements are treated differently from normal gigs. Both the government and the unions get a bit more involved.

If you want to apply, look for "Canada" in the telephone directory of the nearest large city. There should be a visa office that will have the necessary forms. There are slight differences for large groups of entertainers (20 or more), or for live concerts not connected with other commercial activity (like selling liquor). For these two types, the Canadians make special allowances and do not use an employment check. There must, however, be a firm contract for the engagement in Canada.

c. HEADING SOUTH — GOING TO THE U.S.A.

In the U.S. the standard employment test is made when you fill out form MA-250. The Department of Labor gets this, together with a copy of the employment contract. After you and your employer sign the form and attach all required information, you are on your way to the labor clearance. The purpose, as mentioned earlier, is to make sure that a Canadian does not take a job away from an American.

Because of the frequency of cross-the-line gigs, certain geographic areas do not require a labor clearance. Anything within 50 miles of the Canadian border falls into this category.

The U.S.A. issues two types of visas to foreign nationals who work in the U.S. An H-2 visa is the most common. The H-1 visa is for those of "distinguished merit and ability." This must be supported by reviews and other documentation. Before you try for the H-1, remember that *The Beatles* first came to the United States for their famous Ed Sullivan Show on an H-2 visa. The H-1 is reserved for those who are very well known.

It is important to cross the line at your designated port of entry to make sure that all your documentation is available.

After passing the labor test, you still have to go through the immigration check. The U.S. officials have a few more questions than Canadian authorities do.

d. BEFORE YOU GET TO THE BORDER

Although each country has a speedy process that can be used in emergency situations, this fast lane is not for regular engagements. You should anticipate problems well in advance, so you don't have trouble at the last minute.

First, make sure you know who is doing what. If you are signed up for one engagement, check with your employer and make sure the forms are in hand. If you are crossing the line for more than one gig, chances are that your agent will handle the paperwork; but don't leave this to chance. Follow up and make sure that the paper is being prepared, or do it yourself.

You will need a written contract for the engagement, and a copy of it must be submitted with your application. Also handy is a packet of any reviews, which show your standing as an entertainer, and a copy of your union membership card, if applicable. The full names of all members of the group, as well as social security or social insurance numbers, should be attached.

Above all, anticipate that this process will take time. If you are just going to the other country for a vacation, it takes only a few moments at the border. When employment is involved, it takes a lot longer. Plan for this; don't sign a firm contract unless a lot of time is allowed and the contract is subject to immigration approval. Usually the paperwork takes more than a month. Phone your immigration office for details.

All of this can be done without a passport. Neither Canadians nor Americans require a passport to go to the other country. If a member of your group is from a third country, he or she will need a passport. Depending on the country he or she is from, you may have to hire an alternate for the engagement. Check this well in advance.

e. TROUBLE SHOOTING

The policy, but not the rules, change from time to time. Every once in a while, the unions involved in music and the two governments get together to sort things out. Canadians say that too many Americans are coming across the line, and taking away jobs. The Americans, particularly in the northern states, have the same complaint about Canadians. As a result of these meetings, policy sometimes changes.

If you are crossing the line a lot, you may find it helpful to use a good immigration lawyer who will know the current policy and be able to advise you about it. A lawyer may also help you with potential problems.

For example, a prior criminal offence may have substantial bearing on whether or not you are permitted to cross the line. This applies to both the United States and Canada. Also, a false statement on any form puts you into the inadmissible or undesirable classification. Remember that crossing any border is viewed by the host country as a privilege, not a right. You are a guest and they are entitled to refuse you entry if they don't like your previous behavior.

Immigration officers are a suspicious lot, and their suspicion will be focussed on you. Medical problems, past criminal charges, even your attitude when questioned at the border may all play a part. If you anticipate a problem, be prepared. Have your reviews, contract, and government forms with you and ready to present.

Your "roadies" face another problem. Sound technicians, road managers, light men, and other technicians are normally viewed as unessential for the operation of your group. The theory is that you can find another highly qualified technician in the host country who will do the job just as well. Include these personnel in your initial application but don't be surprised if their names are rejected. Unlike yourselves, they are not entertainers and, hence, do not have a unique status under immigration laws. They have to prove their unique status by reference to something peculiar to the group. For example, one roadie may operate a unique sound system that no one else could possibly understand (and you have to prove this). This may qualify your sound technician for entry. Otherwise, be prepared to hire someone across the line.

f. IMMIGRATION

If you plan on working a lot in Canada or the United States, the procedures outlined above for separate visas will normally be insufficient. If this is the case, you should look at the potential of obtaining immigrant status for the country to which you are moving. You do not lose your present citizenship when applying for immigration. As you might expect, those who have been able to use the H-1 status have a preference in this area in the U.S.

Naturally, you will only need to consider this route if you will be getting most, if not all, of your engagements in the other country. Common sense and business sense apply here.

g. TAX CONSIDERATIONS

Both the United States and Canada are parties to a treaty that is aimed at avoiding duplicate taxation. Both countries tax foreign nationals at the time such foreign nationals receive payment. Both countries also tax their own residents annually for worldwide income. If you have already paid the withholding tax in Canada, it comes as a bit of a shock to find that you will be taxed again on the full amount of the monies when you file your U.S. tax return, and vice versa.

To avoid the hassle of applying for refunds later, you have to establish qualifications under the tax treaty. Before you cross the border and receive payment (or have a part of such payment withheld), check with your accountant and obtain the necessary qualification forms for your cross-the-line employer. This will avoid considerable problems when you file your annual return or claim a refund.

Under the treaty you pay no tax in the other country if you agree to report the income and pay the taxes in your home country.

h. TAKING EQUIPMENT ACROSS THE LINE

If you will be crossing the border periodically for engagements, you will have to be prepared to verify ownership of all your equipment. Before you even start out, prepare a list, or inventory, of all the instruments and equipment used by the band, including the van. List the makes, model numbers, serial numbers, and values. Keep this list up-to-date at all times.

Customs officials, because of the nature of their job, assume that you are going to try and sell some of your equipment in their country. Forget the fact that you wouldn't part with your favorite amplifier even if your life depended on it; to the customs officers, it's just another saleable item.

Canadian customs officials are in the habit of requiring bonds for your equipment as it crosses the border. This, in turn, requires a cash security deposit, all of which is intended to ensure that your equipment will return with you to the United States.

For Canadians going to the States, or Americans going to Canada, there are some steps you can take to avoid a hassle.

First, when you have a free day, pack up all the gear in the van and go on down to your local customs office. There is normally one in each town, often next to the post office. Tell the customs official of your country that you are planning to take your equipment to the other country. He or she will go over your equipment list (verified by examining the equipment itself) and complete a "temporary export permit" on a government form. Both of you sign this form.

You can also do this job in your own country just prior to crossing the border, but border crossings are busy places, so if you can do it in your hometown, it's a lot simpler.

If you add equipment before you depart for the other country, get an additional temporary export permit. In Canada, this form is reusable. In the United States, you have to renew it each time you depart the country. However, with your handy band inventory, the process is made much easier.

The purpose of this particular exercise is two-fold. First, Canadian customs may or may not require a bond. If you have the American temporary export permit, they may not insist upon a bond. (By the way, the bond should be equal to 30% of the value of the equipment, which is the amount of duty that would be payable on it if you did intend to sell it in Canada.)

Second, on your return home your temporary export permit provides evidence that you had the equipment when you left and, hence, you won't be charged duty on bringing the equipment back. Some bands have had problems where they couldn't prove that the equipment they had was bought in their home country. The assumption was made that they picked it up cheaply away from home.

If members of your band have additional personal items, (e.g., camera gear), they should get their own temporary export permit as well. This helps when you are coming home. Once again, the purpose is to prove that you had the items when you left the country and did not acquire them abroad.

A second way of avoiding a border hassle over equipment is to purchase a carnet. This is more common in Europe than in the U.S. and Canada. A band that tours often across the line will find this quite a useful item and, after acquiring one, you will be all set to travel internationally as well as in North America.

You obtain your carnet by posting a bond with the Chamber of Commerce. You will be sent some forms that you take to the United States or Canadian customs when you leave your own country. Make sure they stamp the cover and first page with their official seal. When you leave the other country, you complete the exit form and your home country customs officials complete the balance. You forward the remaining forms back to the Chamber of Commerce and they return your deposit.

The purpose of a carnet is rather simple. Because you have already posted a bond you don't have to post another with customs. There are certain limitations to this method that you can check with both customs and the Chamber of Commerce before you proceed.

You can apply for your carnet to the U.S. Chamber of Commerce, Carnet Bureau, or the Canadian Chamber of Commerce. Their office addresses are listed in the Appendix. Write to them for more information, including cost of obtaining a carnet. Remember, it will take time.

When selecting your values for the purposes of either customs or the purchase of a carnet, remember you are not insuring the items. The function of the documents is different, so you can estimate on the low side of their value. But be reasonable. The lower the combined value of all equipment and instruments is, the less will be the deposit required either through customs or the Chamber of Commerce.

i. DRUGS, LIQUOR, AND FIREARMS

If you haven't crossed a border before, be prepared. You can take liquor, but only in limited quantities. Better to pick up what you can at the duty-free shop and leave the rest at home. Both countries have more than adequate supplies.

Drugs are another matter. As you might expect, these are not permitted. The border guards are fully equipped with German Shepherds trained to detect drugs. If they find any, even the smallest morsel, you can say goodbye to the engagement. You may not get another chance. If you indulge, leave it behind. Remember, to the officers at the border you are unusual, and unusual people usually get special interest and treatment. This applies both on the way out, and the way in.

Firearms are another prohibited item. Some may be allowed — check before you arrive at the border. Most are not permitted. If you have a gun, expect a lot of problems when crossing. It doesn't seem worth it to travel with them.

12

LIQUOR AND DRUGS

This chapter may seem a little out of place. Its insertion in this book is not meant to imply that every musician is heavily into alcohol and drugs. Unfortunately, because of the nature of the music business, a musician is exposed to both alcohol and drugs more than the average person. One might even say that this exposure is an occupational risk.

a. LIQUOR

The profits from the sale of alcohol provide one of the major reasons for the current boom in live entertainment. Take a look at the list of engagements you have received. Now, from this list, subtract every club or nightspot that serves alcohol. Are there any left? You cannot underestimate the impact that the sale of alcohol has on your business.

As your list probably shows, if one excludes the sale of alcohol from the live music business, there are relatively few engagements left — high school dances and club dances where the social function is more important, and a limited number of other types of bookings. This doesn't mean that there would be no live music business if prohibition were brought in tomorrow. But there certainly would be a large number of unemployed musicians.

1. Legal age and other drinking laws

One of the first things you should check with your lawyer after the band is formed is whether or not you can perform in a licensed premise if any band member is under the legal drinking age. Most jurisdictions will permit you to perform as long as you don't drink.

If the laws in your area do not allow an underage member to perform, you might have to do some very serious thinking about what type of music or what type of engagements the band can undertake. This doesn't mean that you have to terminate the underage members. What it does mean is that you must be more careful in your selection of engagements and perhaps hire an alternate for those engagements made in licensed establishments.

Some jurisdictions also have rather peculiar rules relating to the use of alcohol by band members. It goes without saying that you don't wish to be drunk or even slightly impeded by alcohol when you are playing. But can you, in fact, even have a drink in the club between sets? You should find out what the rules and regulations are for your jurisdiction. Ask your lawyer or contact an inspector for the local liquor board or liquor authority, listed under state or provincial government in your telephone directory.

Club owners also have different rules concerning drinking while performing. Some provide a drinking allowance for the band; others rise up in righteous horror when a band member goes anywhere near the bar. You are running a business; for you it's not a social occasion, it's a work night. For each engagement, make sure you know the rules of the house before you get into trouble.

Remember, you are professional musicians. If your ability to do the job becomes impaired by alcohol or drugs, will this employer hire you again? Will you be recommended to other establishments? You may be very, very good in your music, but if your potential customers can't rely upon you after the second set, you won't have many future engagements.

2. The audience

Members of your audience will be drinking. This is both a blessing and a curse. It certainly livens up the group but some may take it a bit too far. Every performer has had to deal with a drunk in the audience at one point in his or her career. It's part of the business. Unfortunately, things get a little out of hand from time to time. If a fight breaks out, chances are your equipment will be an early casualty. Drunks have a seemingly endless fascination with electrical outlets and wiring, which means you have a liability problem. Much of this is cured by simply insuring your equipment and obtaining proper liability insurance as is outlined in chapter 8, and by some good planning when setting up. On a practical basis, you and your band members can work out a disaster plan. Talk with other groups and see if they have run into the problems and, if so, what solutions they have come up with.

Remember that in protecting yourselves and your equipment, even against a drunk, you can only use reasonable force. If you go beyond this, you could potentially be charged with assault even though the drunk provoked the attack.

b. DRUGS

Drugs represent an additional problem. As everyone knows, they are illegal. No state or province in North America has legalized marijuana or any of the other hallucinogenic drugs. Forget the street talk you have heard about possession of one joint being okay. You could still be busted. The same applies to cocaine, amphetamines, and any of the illegal or restricted drugs. The law says "you shouldn't have them and you can't use them."

If you are a plumber or a clerk, a criminal charge for drug possession will really not have too much effect. Chances are your employer won't even know. However, as a member of a band, you have other considerations. In some jurisdictions, the liquor laws prohibit any person with a criminal record from being employed in an establishment that serves alcoholic beverages.

Now, remember that list of recent engagements and the number of places that served alcohol? What if these were taken away from you simply because of a bust on a marijuana possession charge? Could you earn a living with the remainder? Not every area is this rigid, but some are. If you plan to indulge, at least check whether this risk is substantial for your business.

If you are going to Canada from the U.S., or to the U.S. from Canada, you will have to obtain a work permit and complete other forms. A criminal charge may jeopardize your ability to cross the border. Both countries have stringent rules concerning work permits. Even one prior conviction for drug possession may affect your ability to cross the line. Yes, John Lennon was permitted into New York even though he had been convicted of a drug offence. But remember, Lennon was prepared to spend an enormous amount of money on legal fees to gain entry. Even then, it was touch and go for a while. If a performer of this stature can find his ability to enter the U.S. impaired by a relatively minor drug charge in England, think of what the U.S. or Canadian authorities will do when confronted with a member of a small, young, travelling band who has a drug charge.

c. LIQUOR, DRUGS, AND CONTRACTS

Never, ever, sign a contract under the influence of alcohol or drugs. You need all your wits about you when you sign a contract. If asked to sign on the dotted line after too much of anything, take a pass — at least for the moment. Invent an excuse ("my lawyer has to read it" is a good one), but don't risk a bad career decision for a short high.

If you do make a mistake, you *may* be able to void the contract, but not without a lot of hassle and legal expense.

d. CONCLUSION

This chapter is not intended as a sermon. The use of alcohol and drugs is a personal decision. However, for entertainers, the decision may have substantial effect on your future career and, therefore, warrants more attention. The legal ramifications can be substantial.

13

AN INTRODUCTION TO COPYRIGHT

a. HISTORY

The law of copyright has a long history. It dates back to 1701 — 75 years before the American Revolution. Prior to that time, artists, musicians, writers, and other people involved in fine arts were protected, only by the difficulty of reproducing their work. The invention and development of the printing press made the distribution of art much easier; but it also made it much more difficult for authors to control and obtain profit from their ideas.

With the mass distribution made possible by printing, writers and other artists needed some protection. The British government recognized this by passing legislation giving writers and artists the right to control and obtain royalties from copies of their works. The *right* to *copy* the original work is a copyright.

Copyright has now become a sophisticated form of law and any problems you run into with it should be referred to your lawyer. The copyright legislation of both the United States and Canada is relatively short and won't take too long to read. You can get a copy of the act and regulations for your own reference from the copyright office (see Appendix). Although much of the language is technical, by reading over the actual legislation you will have a better idea of what the whole system is about.

Over the years, it became necessary to recognize copyright in other countries. For this reason, a number of international conventions or treaties were signed by a variety of countries. The underlying principle of all of these treaties is that a resident of another country will be permitted the same rights to copyright as a national or resident of the country in which registration is sought, and nothing further. If you want full copyright protection in two or more countries, you must register your copyright in two or more countries. Some countries are not members of any of the various conventions and have stricter rules for foreign nationals. Both the United States and Canada are members of several international treaties; both are members of the Universal Copyright Convention.

b. WHAT COPYRIGHT IS ALL ABOUT

The copyright acts of both the United States and Canada give the originator ownership of certain defined types of "works" (including books, music, pictures, and other materials) as long as certain rules are followed. These rules apply even though registration is *not* completed by the writer or originator. They are in effect from the time the work is created.

Copyright is a property right. It gives you ownership, with some limitations. A "concept" or "idea" is a little too nebulous to be protected. Imagine what would happen if the first person to conceive of a love ballad had the copyright to all love ballads that followed. As a result, a concept or idea cannot be protected; only the tangible form in which the concept or idea is expressed can be protected by copyright. The name of your group or the name of a song, original and distinctive as they may be, normally cannot be copyrighted. Neither have sufficient content to be protected. (Remember, though, that your group name can be protected by trademark.)

Artistic merit is not a requirement of copyright. The concept or idea must be original and reduced to some tangible form. Now, it is quite possible that two people have exactly the same idea at exactly the same time. As long as both can show that they didn't know what the other was doing, both would be entitled to the copyright of the same material.

This original idea has to be put into some concrete format. Merely thinking of melody, attaching words to it, and singing it in public does not qualify. You have to write the song down. The melody line as well as the lyrics must be written down. In Canada you can register the harmony as well as the melody. In the United States the song may be recorded on tape or record instead of being written.

Copyright gives you the exclusive property right to use your song for a profit. It is really a "bundle of rights." This bundle includes the right to reproduce the song, prepare derivative works, distribute copies to the public (by way of record, sheet music or otherwise), perform the song in public, and many other rights.

There are also certain exemptions to copyright. Two common exemptions are "fair use" and "not-for-profit." Both of these, as with the other exemptions, are rather limited. Fair use, for example, would include using your property for criticism, research, or teaching. "Not-for-profit" might include religious, charitable, or government usage. The exclusions or limitations on copyright are set out in both the United States and Canada copyright acts. Check with your lawyer if you have any questions about either the rights included within copyright or the exclusions from it. You can also refer to some of the books listed in the Bibliography.

c. OWNERSHIP OF COPYRIGHT

As a rule, copyright in a song "vests" in, or is owned by, the originator, or songwriter, at the time the song is created. The person who creates and conceives the song is the person who owns the copyright. The originator then has a choice of claiming "common law" copyright (sometimes known as "poor man's copyright"), or registering copyright in the material with the government, or doing both. At this stage, the music has been reduced to a concrete format but may or may not have been published. (See more on publication in chapter 15.)

If you write a song as an employee of someone else, ownership is viewed differently. Generally, if you are an employee and employed *for the purpose of writing songs*, ownership in the song remains with your employer. This would be reflected in the necessary copyright notice. To change this, a specific contract between you and your employer is necessary.

If someone has specially commissioned a song from you, the rules are slightly different in the United States and Canada. In the United States, you would still be the owner of the copyright. In Canada, the person who commissioned you would own the copyright. To avoid any confusion, the agreement between you and the person employing you or commissioning the song should include a specific paragraph dealing with the matter of copyright. It could go either way or could be joint. The copyright notice should then reflect the specific terms of your agreement.

d. THE COPYRIGHT NOTICE

To protect your rights, ensure that a copyright notice is printed on or affixed to any copy of your song. The copyright notice has three parts, the first of which is a copyright symbol. The copyright symbol is a "C" in a circle, printed as: ©.

The next two elements of the copyright notice are the year in which the song was published and the name of the owner. If your song hasn't been published, use the year the song was written. Where two or more people helped create the song, all names should appear on the notice; this is called joint copyright as each owns an undivided part of the whole right. If these people have a common company, then the company can become the owner of the copyright. Unless your band has incorporated, the name of your band should not be used as the name of the copyright owner. If you have to, name all members of the band as joint owners.

In the United States, the phrase "All Rights Reserved" should form part of the copyright notice. Thus, the complete copyright notice would be:

© 1985 Randy Baker
　All Rights Reserved

or

© 1985 Randy Baker and Larry Hop
　All Rights Reserved

Instead of the symbol, you can use the expression "Copyright" or its abbreviation "Copr." However, as the word and its abbreviation are not internationally recognized, use of the copyright symbol is recommended. If you wish, you may use both the word as well as the symbol.

In Canada, this copyright notice is not strictly required, but you should use it anyway, for better protection.

If you do not add the copyright notice to your songs, you will probably lose any protection that copyright might give you. The law in this area is complex and should be discussed with your lawyer. If you lose copyright, your song becomes part of the "public domain." At this stage, the law says that the song belongs to the public and not to its originator. It's rather like giving a gift to charity, but without a tax deduction.

1. Where to use the notice

Even if you do not register the copyright, it is important that the copyright notice be on every piece of music you produce. Get in the habit of putting it down. It should appear on the first page (if you want to be safe, on every page) of a lead sheet for the song, that is, sheet music using normal musical notation. Just by affixing the symbol, you claim your legal rights. It shows you own the song you have created.

If one member of your band has some musical background and can write out music, one of his or her jobs can be to do up a lead sheet for each piece of material written by members of the band, with the notice attached. Get in the habit of doing this. After all, if you do write a hit like *Sounds of Silence*, you want both the credit and the money that comes from it. Where two or more members of your band make up a song, but are not equal owners, do up a quick agreement in writing. This can be nothing more than a document with the name of the song, the division of the ownership, and the names and signatures of all concerned.

2. Demo tape and the copyright notice

If you are circulating demo tapes as part of your promo kit, the tape itself should also display the complete copyright notice on both sides. The tape, and the songs on it, each have their own separate copyrights. If you have an incorporated company for your band, use the company name. If not, use the names of all members of the band.

If the songs on the tape are original, you might consider specifying this and giving the copyright particulars of the songs on a sheet inserted in your promo kit (this is much like the copyright notices displayed for each selection on a record). Look at the records in your collection — they will provide an easy guide.

e. COPYRIGHT BY MAIL

Although a copyright notice gives the year of creation, it is limited in its protection. One method of increasing protection is known as "copyright by mail." You can prepare a lead sheet or cassette tape of any original material and mail it to yourself by registered mail. When the letter is delivered, do not open it. Simply file it away in a safe place for future reference. You may even consider storing these letters in a safety deposit box at your local bank. Keep an extra copy of the song in your files for quick reference, and so you know what is in the envelope.

Be sure to include the name and date of writing of the song on the outside of the envelope. After a while, you might collect a number of these envelopes; you don't want to have to open them to find out what's in them.

What's the point of this exercise? By sending yourself a registered letter, you have fixed the date of the song. The post office, in its obliging fashion, has stamped the outside of the envelope and recorded its delivery. You are creating evidence for a possible legal battle, if someone steals your song. As evidence, this isn't too bad. It's not as good as registration, but it is at least some evidence of the date you wrote the song. Remember, don't open the envelope. The minute you do, any additional protection you have achieved is lost.

One drawback to this method is that you actually have control of the envelope. People have been known to steam open envelopes and some have successfully resealed them without any evidence of tampering. You could write your name or initials on the flap of the envelope as further evidence next to where the post office has obligingly stamped it. But even so, you will no doubt be questioned in court and the other side will raise the issue of control.

To avoid this potential problem, you can go one step further and send the letter directly to your lawyer with instructions to hold all such letters received in a safety deposit box. If it goes to court at a later date, your lawyer will be able to file an affidavit stating that the letter was received on a specific date and was retained in the safety deposit box, unopened, since that date. Now, not only have you sent the letter but it has been sent to an uninterested party and it is, accordingly, better evidence if things come to a court battle. You have just added another witness to testify on your behalf.

Some songwriters use the service of the Songwriters' Resources and Services (SRS) or the American Protection Service (APS) for copyright protection. For a fee substantially less than the normal American or Canadian copyright registration fee, SRS or APS will record the date your material was received and place it in a vault. Later, if a court action results, one of their staff will retrieve your material from their vault and be able to give evidence concerning its receipt and storage. Write to SRS or APS at the addresses given in the Appendix for a schedule of their fees for this service.

f. COPYRIGHT INFRINGEMENT

The principle behind all of these methods is to fix the date on which your song was written. You are basically manufacturing evidence on your own behalf for a future court case. You are creating better evidence when you use your lawyer's office, SRS, or APS as a depository of the material. However, good as these procedures are, they are not equivalent to registration of your copyright. Before you can commence an action for copyright infringement, you must have registered your copyright with the copyright office in the U.S. or in Canada. While you may be successful in your action, the effect of non-registration makes

111

your case much weaker. It will also eliminate the "statutory damages" in such an action and your claim for legal fees if the actual infringement has occurred prior to the date of your formal copyright registration for the song. Copyright registration is discussed in the next chapter.

Once you have completed your copyright notice and registered your copyright, you are in a position to protect it. Legally, with some exceptions, this means that you can prevent anybody else from using your material without paying for it. You can also sue them and recover damages from them if they do use your material without your consent.

A person who uses your material without consent is said to be infringing upon your copyright. If someone writes a song that sounds just like yours or has the same title or similar lyrics, you have to show two things to recover successfully in a copyright infringement action. These two elements are similarity and access.

1. Similarity

The first element in proving infringement is determining similarity of your music to the other piece. Remember, you are only concerned with the melody line, not the harmonies or arrangements. If you suspect that another piece of music has been based on yours, you will undoubtedly need the help of a musicologist or someone who has some advanced musical knowledge.

The first step is to write out the melody line of your song on standard music sheets. Then transpose the melody line from the other song to the same key and write that out as well. Use two staff lines so that your song appears directly above the other song. This process visually reduces the differences between the two songs to the melody line and, by using the same key, removes differences that result from different keys. What you are left with are the bare bones of the melody, both set down in the same key.

Next, look at the structure of the music. Is it the same? Are the same notes or phrases used? Is the timing similar in the melody line? The more notes on the combined sheet that are similar, the more likelihood there is that sufficient similarity exists to justify an infringement action. If lyrics are involved, similarity between the structure of these words will also point the way toward the necessary similarity.

To show infringement, you must be able to demonstrate that the melody of the other song is very similar to yours. Alternatively, the lyrics may be substantially the same, or similar. Or both portions of the melody and the lyrics may be similar. As you cannot copyright the title, a similarity between your title and that of the other song is, at best, support to the main argument.

In establishing the similarity with the melody line, it is not enough for the notes to be in the same position; sequentially, the notes must follow a particular pattern. As well, the value of the notes, which establishes the rhythm, is also important in establishing a similarity.

Now, obviously, you can have melodies that sound similar, that have the same tempo, instrumentation, and other qualities in common but which are not infringements of each other. Important as these other elements are and similar as they may make the song sound, as long as the lyrics or melody are not similar, infringement does not exist. In recent years, the particular treatment and tempo of certain songs have spawned a number of imitations. Although these imitations sound similar, the melody is substantially different and, hence, there is no infringement upon the initial copyright.

2. Access

If you can show similarity, you then have the hurdle of proving access. Remember that two people could, in theory, obtain copyright to the same melody independently. Accordingly, in a case of copyright infringement, you must show that the other songwriter had access to your material. If your material has been recorded and broadcast, you can show access simply by the fact that your song was being played at the same time the other person wrote the infringing piece. The George Harrison case, discussed below, is a good example of this situation.

In other instances, you may be able to show that a demo tape or record was forwarded to a particular publisher and that the publisher also acts for the other songwriter. There are myriad possibilities.

3. Intention

Some people believe, erroneously, that you have to *intend* to copy another person's material for infringement to take place. This is not true. Your intention, at the time the copy is made, is not relevant. Even accidental copying can be covered by an infringement action, as long as similarity and access can be proven.

So, remember the two basic tests: sufficient similarity, and access. These two factors will establish your basic copyright infringement action.

4. *The Beatles* go to court

In 1962, a group known as *The Chiffons* recorded a song called *He's So Fine*. The song made the charts both in the United States and England. In the United States, it went up to Number One. In England, it was in the Top 20.

In 1970, George Harrison came out with a song called *My Sweet Lord*. This song also became quite popular. The trouble was, though, that the two songs seemed fairly similar. Bright Tunes Music Corporation, the owner of the copyright and the publisher of *He's So Fine*, sued Harrison for copyright infringement.

The case has become a classic in considering copyright infringement. The words of the song don't have any similarity; even the theme and mood of the two songs are completely different. However, Bright Tunes was able to show that the music, reduced to the simple basic melody line, was almost identical. Constructed basically of two separate phrases, both songs repeat the same pattern and bridge. On this basis, Bright Tunes had passed the first test. But what about access?

The court found that there had been access. It was prepared to infer that Harrison would have listened to all songs on the British charts in 1963, including *He's So Fine*. He therefore had the necessary access to the material. In this case, the court did not hold that Harrison knew he was copying the song when he wrote *My Sweet Lord*. Rather, because of the similarity and the access, the court decided that Harrison had subconsciously copied the tune when he wrote his song. The court ordered Harrison to pay the royalties he received to the publisher of the original song.

5. Injunctions and other relief

In addition to the basic copyright infringement action, a copyright owner may also take additional steps to protect his or her rights.

One weapon in the arsenal is an injunction. An injunction is an order made by a court that prevents or forbids some form of conduct. If you find out that someone is intending to distribute copies of a record with your song on it and has not obtained a licence from you, an injunction will prevent the distribution of the records. If another group is going to use your name in a performance, you can prevent them from doing so by court order.

An injunction is useful as you can prevent something from happening before it happens. If the action complained of is one of a series of events, you can stop future events of the same type. Or, if some records have been produced with your song on them, or someone makes a tape of one of your performances and tries to sell it, the material may be impounded and possibly destroyed.

Pirates risk a further penalty. Where infringement occurs for commercial gain, there may be a criminal penalty of up to one year in jail and a $10,000 fine. In the case of sound recordings, the fine may be increased to $250,000. Further offences can result in higher sentences and fines. In addition, in criminal cases, the offending copies as well as the equipment used to manufacture them can be destroyed. A willful infringement will also pay substantially higher damages in a civil suit.

Infringement action must be brought by the owner of the copyright. This could be either the writer, the publisher, or the record producer. Note that this list does not include the performer.

Certain groups have developed very unique styles and harmonies for the presentation of their acts. *The Beach Boys* sound like *The Beach Boys*; no one else sounds just like *Jefferson Starship*. It's pretty hard not to recognize the distinctive styles of particular performers. Unfortunately, a performer cannot copyright the way material is presented. In your act, you may imitate as many groups as you wish and there is nothing anyone can do about it. By the same token, if you achieve tremendous success and become well known, you can't prevent others from imitating your style. The style of a performance, or the way in which it is delivered, cannot be copyrighted. At most, a passing off action might be commenced, but only if the other performer uses the same name as well as other attributes of your band.

14

COPYRIGHT REGISTRATION

In the preceding chapter, we explored ways of protecting your song without formally applying for copyright registration. It should be stressed that all of the "common law" ways of protecting your work are less effective than formal copyright registration. Indeed, given the benefits that flow from formal registration, the only rational reasons for not proceeding are simply those of cost or complexity — both of which are overrated.

a. AMERICAN COPYRIGHT REGISTRATION

Just in time for the American Bicentennial, the United States government passed a new and substantially modified copyright act. This new act went into effect on January 1, 1978.

Under the preceding legislation, copyright was quite a mess. Control over copyright was split between the federal and state governments. The state governments had control over copyright between the time you wrote your song and the time it was published; after publication, the federal law took over. This, and other aspects of the old legislation, created considerable problems and confusion. In addition, the old act had been firmly anchored in outdated technology. It had been passed prior to the technological advances of the 1950s, 1960s, and 1970s.

1. What can be registered?

In a nutshell, the purpose of copyright registration for a song is to record an original musical creation, which gives certain statutory rights to the songwriter. As mentioned, you cannot copyright a title or short phrase of song, nor can you copyright the name of your band. The original idea that copyright seeks to protect must be longer than a mere title, it must have substantial length and content. When it comes to music, this simply means that the song can be copyrighted, but not the song's title. For example, there are many songs titled *I'm In Love*, and you can make up another one under the same title if you wish. Your title would not be protected, but the lyrics and music, as original material, would be.

For registration, your song must also be fixed in some tangible form before you can proceed. This can be done with a lead sheet (i.e., the song has to be put down on paper using normal musical notations) or a cassette tape, which makes the process a lot easier.

U.S. copyright registration of a song is limited to two specific ingredients: the lyrics (or the words of the song), and the melody (the actual tune of the song). It does not cover instrumentation, tempo, the key, or other necessary elements of your music. Nor does it protect either the title or the subject matter of the song.

2. Benefits of registration

The first and most obvious benefit of registration is that you date the time of your song's creation with the official government recorder, the copyright office. It is possible to fix the time by the other methods discussed in the previous chapter, but copyright registration provides more and better protection.

Once you have registered your copyright to the song, it gives what is known as a *prima facie* presumption. The presumption is that you own the copyright and the material the copyright represents. Insofar as court cases are concerned, this is very important. If you get into an actual court case and have not registered your copyright, you first have to try to prove when you wrote the song and what form it took. If you have copyrighted your material, you simply file the copyright registration which, in and of itself, "proves" your ownership.

The person you are suing, must then show that there is not sufficient similarity or that he or she did not have access. This may not sound like much but, in a courtroom, it can be very important. (See the preceding chapter for more on copyright infringement.)

Another benefit is that you can commence a copyright infringement action only if you have completed the registration process. If you sue for infringement, you will hope to win damages, or cash. If you have not registered your material, the amount of damages has to be proven. For example, you would have to prove that you lost $5,000 because someone infringed upon your copyright. This has to be proved in a court of law and can be difficult and expensive.

A further problem is that the level of these damages may be quite small in proportion to the cost of commencing this type of action. If you have registered, however, the statute sets out certain statutory damages to which you are entitled. Thus, without proving any actual cash loss, you can still recover a fairly large amount of money. For innocent infringement, the statutory damages are $250 to $10,000; if the infringement is willful, the maximum amount per infringement increases to $50,000.

On a practical basis, the net effect of copyright registration in an infringement action is that your costs are reduced and the defendant's are increased. In most legal actions, both parties pay their own legal costs. So, if your attorney costs you $20,000 for the action and you only recover $50,000 from the defendant, you get $30,000. But if you have registered your copyright, you are also awarded costs, which means the amount of reasonable legal fees and disbursements that you have paid out. In such a case, if you recovered $50,000 that would be your damages. You would also recover a further $20,000 (assuming that figure was reasonable) to cover your legal costs. The defendant would, therefore, pay you a total of $70,000 and you would keep $50,000 (subject to whatever arrangements you had made with your lawyer). That's a considerable increase in your recovery.

3. How to apply

You can write or phone the copyright office of the United States (see Appendix) and they will send you the necessary forms.

You must use the forms provided by the copyright office. You cannot type them yourself or photocopy them or reproduce them in any other fashion. You have to use the forms that the copyright office will freely send you.

Let's assume you have written one song and wish to copyright it. The form you want from the copyright office is called Form PA. (PA stands for performing arts.) When you order this form from the copyright office, it comes complete with instructions. The instructions are fairly straightforward and easy to follow (see Sample #3). One of the blanks is entitled "Nature of this Work." In this regard, if you have written lyrics only, you would fill in "Song Lyrics." If you are registering the melody line, you would simply put in "Music." A song with music and lyrics would become "Words and Music." In Part 2, you would fill in "Name of Author" with your own name. The rest of the form is fairly self-explanatory and, fortunately, the attached instructions are quite clear. If you need help, get your lawyer to guide you through the questions the first time through.

The actual form is only two pages long. If you need additional space (for example, where all four members of your band have contributed toward the song), you can get what is called a "Continuation Sheet for Form PA" from the copyright office. Remember, you have to use the form provided by the government. You can't simply make one up on your own.

Now that you have completed the form, you have only a few steps left to complete. Remember, your song has to be in some tangible form. Before the new act was passed, this had to be by way of lead sheet. Now, you can also make up a cassette of the song (more of this later) and use this as an alternate to the lead sheet.

SAMPLE #3
COPYRIGHT FORM PA (U.S.)

FORM PA
UNITED STATES COPYRIGHT OFFICE

REGISTRATION NUMBER

PA   PAU

EFFECTIVE DATE OF REGISTRATION

Month   Day   Year

DO NOT WRITE ABOVE THIS LINE. IF YOU NEED MORE SPACE, USE A SEPARATE CONTINUATION SHEET.

1 **TITLE OF THIS WORK ▼**

Moody City

PREVIOUS OR ALTERNATIVE TITLES ▼

Vancouver

NATURE OF THIS WORK ▼ See instructions

Words and music

2 **NAME OF AUTHOR▼**
a Simon Glick

DATES OF BIRTH AND DEATH
Year Born ▼ Year Died ▼
1946

Was this contribution to the work a "work made for hire"?
☐ Yes
☒ No

AUTHOR'S NATIONALITY OR DOMICILE
Name of Country
OR { Citizen of ▶ Canada
{ Domiciled in ▶ Canada

WAS THIS AUTHOR'S CONTRIBUTION TO THE WORK
Anonymous?   ☐ Yes ☒ No
Pseudonymous? ☐ Yes ☒ No
If the answer to either of these questions is "Yes," see detailed instructions.

NOTE

Under the law, the "author" of a "work made for hire" is generally the employer, not the employee (see instructions). For any part of this work that was "made for hire" check "Yes" in the space provided, give the employer (or other person for whom the work was prepared) as "Author" of that part, and leave the space for dates of birth and death blank.

NATURE OF AUTHORSHIP Briefly describe nature of the material created by this author in which copyright is claimed. ▼
Words and music

NAME OF AUTHOR ▼
b

DATES OF BIRTH AND DEATH
Year Born ▼ Year Died ▼

Was this contribution to the work a "work made for hire"?
☐ Yes
☐ No

AUTHOR'S NATIONALITY OR DOMICILE
Name of Country
OR { Citizen of ▶
{ Domiciled in ▶

WAS THIS AUTHOR'S CONTRIBUTION TO THE WORK
Anonymous?   ☐ Yes ☐ No
Pseudonymous? ☐ Yes ☐ No
If the answer to either of these questions is "Yes," see detailed instructions.

NATURE OF AUTHORSHIP Briefly describe nature of the material created by this author in which copyright is claimed. ▼

NAME OF AUTHOR ▼
c

DATES OF BIRTH AND DEATH
Year Born ▼ Year Died ▼

Was this contribution to the work a "work made for hire"?
☐ Yes
☐ No

AUTHOR'S NATIONALITY OR DOMICILE
Name of Country
OR { Citizen of ▶
{ Domiciled in ▶

WAS THIS AUTHOR'S CONTRIBUTION TO THE WORK
Anonymous?   ☐ Yes ☐ No
Pseudonymous? ☐ Yes ☐ No
If the answer to either of these questions is "Yes," see detailed instructions.

NATURE OF AUTHORSHIP Briefly describe nature of the material created by this author in which copyright is claimed. ▼

3 **YEAR IN WHICH CREATION OF THIS WORK WAS COMPLETED** This information must be given in all cases.
1985 ◀ Year

DATE AND NATION OF FIRST PUBLICATION OF THIS PARTICULAR WORK Complete this information ONLY if this work has been published.
Month ▶   Day ▶   Year ▶
◀ Nation

4 **COPYRIGHT CLAIMANT(S)** Name and address must be given even if the claimant is the same as the author given in space 2.▼

Simon Glick
1234 Main Street
Southtown, B.C. Canada V1K 2G1

See instructions before completing this space.

TRANSFER If the claimant(s) named here in space 4 are different from the author(s) named in space 2, give a brief statement of how the claimant(s) obtained ownership of the copyright.▼

APPLICATION RECEIVED
ONE DEPOSIT RECEIVED
TWO DEPOSITS RECEIVED
REMITTANCE NUMBER AND DATE

DO NOT WRITE HERE OFFICE USE ONLY

MORE ON BACK ▶ • Complete all applicable spaces (numbers 5-9) on the reverse side of this page.
• See detailed instructions.   • Sign the form at line 8.

DO NOT WRITE HERE
Page 1 of _____ pages

121

SAMPLE #3 — Continued

DO NOT WRITE ABOVE THIS LINE. IF YOU NEED MORE SPACE, USE A SEPARATE CONTINUATION SHEET.

PREVIOUS REGISTRATION   Has registration for this work, or for an earlier version of this work, already been made in the Copyright Office?
☐ Yes ☒ No   If your answer is "Yes," why is another registration being sought? (Check appropriate box) ▼
☐ This is the first published edition of a work previously registered in unpublished form.
☐ This is the first application submitted by this author as copyright claimant.
☐ This is a changed version of the work, as shown by space 6 on this application.
If your answer is "Yes," give: **Previous Registration Number ▼**   **Year of Registration ▼**

5

DERIVATIVE WORK OR COMPILATION   Complete both space 6a & 6b for a derivative work; complete only 6b for a compilation.
a. **Preexisting Material**   Identify any preexisting work or works that this work is based on or incorporates. ▼

N/A

b. **Material Added to This Work**   Give a brief, general statement of the material that has been added to this work and in which copyright is claimed.▼

N/A

6

See instructions
before completing
this space

DEPOSIT ACCOUNT   If the registration fee is to be charged to a Deposit Account established in the Copyright Office, give name and number of Account.
Name ▼   **Account Number ▼**

N/A   N/A

7

CORRESPONDENCE   Give name and address to which correspondence about this application should be sent.   Name/Address/Apt/City/State/Zip ▼

Simon Glick
1234 Main St.
Southtown, B.C.
Canada V1K 2G1

Area Code & Telephone Number ▶   (604) 599-2307

Be sure to
give your
daytime phone
◀ number

CERTIFICATION*   I, the undersigned, hereby certify that I am the
Check only one ▼
☐ author
☐ other copyright claimant
☐ owner of exclusive right(s)
☐ authorized agent of _____
              Name of author or other copyright claimant, or owner of exclusive right(s) ▲

of the work identified in this application and that the statements made
by me in this application are correct to the best of my knowledge.

Typed or printed name and date ▼ If this is a published work, this date must be the same as or later than the date of publication given in space 3.

Simon Glick   date ▶ July 5, 198–

☞ **Handwritten signature (X) ▼**

8

**MAIL
CERTIFI-
CATE TO**

Name ▼
Simon Glick

Number/Street/Apartment Number ▼
1234 Main St.

City/State/ZIP ▼
Southtown, B.C.   Canada   V1K 2G1

**Certificate
will be
mailed in
window
envelope**

Have you:
• Completed all necessary
  spaces?
• Signed your application in space
  8?
• Enclosed check or money order
  for $10 payable to *Register of
  Copyrights?*
• Enclosed your deposit material
  with the application and fee?
MAIL TO: Register of Copyrights,
Library of Congress, Washington,
D.C. 20559.

9

* 17 U.S.C. § 506(e): Any person who knowingly makes a false representation of a material fact in the application for copyright registration provided for by section 409, or in any written statement filed in connection with the application, shall be fined not more than $2,500.

☆ U.S. GOVERNMENT PRINTING OFFICE: 1981: 355–306

Nov. 1981–700,000

With your form and lead sheets or tapes in hand, all you need is a $10 money order or check. Put your application form, two copies of your song (the lead sheets or tapes)*, and the money order or check into an envelope, and mail to the copyright office.

Because of the sheer volume that the copyright office has to contend with, expect a delay of five months before you get back your certificate bearing a registration number. Don't be too worried about this. Your material is actually dated by the copyright office on the date they receive it. Your certificate is in effect "backdated" to the date your material was received and not the date the actual registration process was completed.

4. Multiple registration

One way of cutting costs is to register more than one song with the same application. Gather all your songs together, either by lead sheets or by cassette tapes. You have to put them under one title, so call the whole set of assembled songs something like "Walker, Randy — Collected Works — Volume I." This would go in the space for "Title of Work" on Form PA. Keep a list of the songs you have registered under this title with you or, if you wish, use a continuation sheet from the copyright office to list these just for convenience. Once again, put the form, the two copies, and the $10 fee in the envelope and send it off.

One of the problems with multiple registration is trying to break out one song from the set at a later date. It requires more paperwork, but by that time you probably have somebody who wants to buy your song, so you shouldn't mind the extra work! Use Form CA for this job (see Sample #4). This form instructs the copyright office to register the songs separately. The fee is $10 plus 50¢ for each title.

If you use multiple registration, remember that the title of your song will be "Walker, Randy — Collected Works — Volume I." Now, that's quite a mouthful. The copyright

---

*One copy if the work has not been published.

office computer will not isolate the individual songs and their titles, only the title of the collected works. Keep your own list of the songs with your registration certificate.

5. Registration by tape or record

As mentioned earlier, lead sheets used to be the only way to register copyright. Now you can use cassette tapes or phonograph records. If you use tapes or records, try to follow a procedure that will assist the copyright office in indexing the material.

Start off each tape or record by an announcement which ties the tape to the form you have completed. For example, "This tape is submitted for copyright registration purposes by Randy Walker (spell out your name if it is difficult), residing at 12486 Hastings Street, Seattle, Washington, U.S.A., 10086. It is filed with the copyright office, Washington, D.C. in 1985. I am the author of the words and music of the song that follows."

Using this type of introduction, you properly identify the material on the tape. If you are registering more than one song, you should add, "There are 10 songs on the tape that follow, all of which are collectively registered under the name 'Walker, Randy — Collected Works — Volume I (1985).'"

Before each song, use a phrase something like, "This is song number one" and the title of the song.

After this introduction, put the song onto the tape. Don't get too fancy — remember, the copyright office is not interested in harmony, only in the melody and lyrics. Sing the song in a clear voice accompanying yourself on the piano or guitar. Keep the accompaniment simple. Don't clutter the tape up; stick to the basics.

6. Registration of sound recording and other protection

If you want to go further with your protection, ask for Form SR, instead of Form PA. On this form, you register not only the words and music, but also the sound recording (that's what the SR stands for). The actual recording has a

SAMPLE #4
COPYRIGHT FORM CA
(U.S.)

FORM CA
UNITED STATES COPYRIGHT OFFICE

REGISTRATION NUMBER

| TX | TXU | PA | PAU | VA | VAU | SR | SRU | RE |

Effective Date of Supplementary Registration

. . . .
MONTH   DAY   YEAR

DO NOT WRITE ABOVE THIS LINE. FOR COPYRIGHT OFFICE USE ONLY

(A)
Basic Instructions

TITLE OF WORK:
Windy City

REGISTRATION NUMBER OF BASIC REGISTRATION:
1765430

YEAR OF BASIC REGISTRATION:
1985

NAME(S) OF AUTHOR(S):
Simon Glick

NAME(S) OF COPYRIGHT CLAIMANT(S):
Simon Glick

(B)
Correction

LOCATION AND NATURE OF INCORRECT INFORMATION IN BASIC REGISTRATION:
Line Number ....7...... Line Heading or Description . Correspondence ....

INCORRECT INFORMATION AS IT APPEARS IN BASIC REGISTRATION:
1234 Main Street
Southtown, B.C.   Canada   V1K 2G1

CORRECTED INFORMATION:
4351 Turnip Row
West Langley, B.C.   Canada   V3R 2S9

EXPLANATION OF CORRECTION: (Optional)
Move of residence

(C)
Amplification

LOCATION AND NATURE OF INFORMATION IN BASIC REGISTRATION TO BE AMPLIFIED:
Line Number ....--...... Line Heading or Description .....--..................................

AMPLIFIED INFORMATION:
N/A

EXPLANATION OF AMPLIFIED INFORMATION: (Optional)
N/A

125

SAMPLE #4 — Continued

	EXAMINED BY:	FORM CA RECEIVED:	FOR COPYRIGHT OFFICE USE ONLY
	CHECKED BY:		
	CORRESPONDENCE: ☐ YES	REMITTANCE NUMBER AND DATE:	
	REFERENCE TO THIS REGISTRATION ADDED TO BASIC REGISTRATION: ☐ YES ☐ NO	DEPOSIT ACCOUNT FUNDS USED: ☐	

DO NOT WRITE ABOVE THIS LINE. FOR COPYRIGHT OFFICE USE ONLY

CONTINUATION OF: (Check which) ☐ PART B OR ☐ PART C

N/A

(D)
Continuation

DEPOSIT ACCOUNT: If the registration fee is to be charged to a Deposit Account established in the Copyright Office, give name and number of Account:

Name   N/A   Account Number   N/A

(E)
Deposit Account and Mailing Instructions

CORRESPONDENCE: Give name and address to which correspondence should be sent:

Name   Simon Glick   Apt. No.

Address   4351 Turnip Row   West Langley   B.C.   Canada   V3R 2S9
(Number and Street)   (City)   (State)   (ZIP Code)

CERTIFICATION ✱ I, the undersigned, hereby certify that I am the: (Check one)

☒ author ☐ other copyright claimant ☐ owner of exclusive right(s) ☐ authorized agent of: ....
(Name of author or other copyright claimant, or owner of exclusive right(s))

of the work identified in this application and that the statements made by me in this application are correct to the best of my knowledge.

Handwritten signature: (X) *Simon Glick*

Typed or printed name.   Simon Glick

Date: April 1, 198-

✱ 17 U.S.C. §506(e): FALSE REPRESENTATION. Any person who knowingly makes a false representation of a material fact in the application for copyright registration provided for by section 409, or in any written statement filed in connection with the application, shall be fined not more than $2,500.

(F)
Certification (Application must be signed)

| Simon Glick |
| (Name) |
| 4351 Turnip Row |
| (Number, Street and Apartment Number) |
| West Langley   B.C.   Canada   V3R 2S9 |
| (City)   (State)   (ZIP code) |

MAIL CERTIFICATE TO

(Certificate will be mailed in window envelope)

(G)
Address for Return of Certificate

different copyright from the words and music. Record producers usually register a record using the Form SR. Note how these rights overlap. The songs are copyrighted and then the album containing a number of songs is also copyrighted. See Sample #5 for an example of Form SR.

If you have come up with a striking design for the cover of your album or record, or if your record has been reproduced with a photograph or drawing on it, the jacket and/or record can be registered separately. Use Form VA (for visual arts) if you are primarily concerned with the visual aspects, or Form TX (the TX stands for texts) if you are interested in protecting the written words on the jacket itself but not necessarily the jacket's design. (See Samples #6 and #7).

7. Duration and public domain

Now that you have registered your copyright, you should consider how long this right will last. Under the present legislation, your copyright will continue for your lifetime plus 50 years after that. If two or more members of your band have written a song, the 50-year period starts with the death of the last survivor. If you have registered the song in the name of your company, copyright lasts for 100 years from the date the song was created, or 75 years from publication, whichever occurs first.

After the copyright period is over, your work becomes public domain. This can also happen if you fail to register. Public domain is like a charitable gift, anyone can use your material without paying you a cent for it.

8. Transfer

You can transfer one or all of the components of copyright to someone else. This transfer can be for a specified period of time and could depend on performance. The Songwriter's Guild contract, for example, contains a transfer of a copyright to your publisher but a reversion of the ownership to you if the publisher fails to perform as required within a set period of time.

If you do transfer some or all of your copyright to someone else, a formal transfer document must be signed by you and a copy of this document filed with the copyright office. This will normally be done by your music publisher.

9. The termination process

Although it has substantially changed from the old legislation, the Copyright Act does contain a termination provision allowing you to end a transfer. A transfer of your copyright normally lasts for 35 years. Assuming you are still alive, you can then get the rights to the song back. If you are not, your heirs can get it back.

Because the termination rules are rather complex, the termination process should be reviewed by your lawyer. You have to give a formal notice to the person who has the copyright. This notice must be in writing and there are specific time rules about when the notice is served. If you don't follow all the rules, the termination is not valid and your original transfer of the rights continues.

10. Publication

To be published, your work must be distributed to the public. Examples of publication are record sales or sheet music sales. Reproduction of your work does not constitute publication. For example, if you make a number of cassettes of your songs and forward these cassettes to music publishers, it isn't publication because your demo tape is not intended for public distribution.

Two copies of all published works (whether or not copyright is registered) must be deposited with the Library of Congress. If you have applied for copyright, there is no need to send additional copies for this purpose. However, if you have not, the requirement to file with the Library of Congress must still be met.

The odd thing is that failure to file with the Library of Congress does not affect your copyright. It does, however, make you subject to a fine for non-deposit.

SAMPLE #5
COPYRIGHT FORM SR
(U.S.)

FORM SR
UNITED STATES COPYRIGHT OFFICE

REGISTRATION NUMBER

SR _____ SRU _____

EFFECTIVE DATE OF REGISTRATION

Month _____ Day _____ Year _____

DO NOT WRITE ABOVE THIS LINE. IF YOU NEED MORE SPACE, USE A SEPARATE CONTINUATION SHEET.

1 **TITLE OF THIS WORK ▼**

Windy City

PREVIOUS OR ALTERNATIVE TITLES ▼

N/A

NATURE OF MATERIAL RECORDED ▼ See instructions

☒ Musical ☐ Musical-Dramatic
☐ Dramatic ☐ Literary
☐ Other _____

2 **NAME OF AUTHOR ▼**

a   Simon Glick

DATES OF BIRTH AND DEATH
Year Born ▼ 1946   Year Died ▼

Was this contribution to the work a "work made for hire"?
☐ Yes ☒ No

AUTHOR'S NATIONALITY OR DOMICILE
Name of Country
OR { Citizen of ▶ Canada
Domiciled in ▶ Canada

WAS THIS AUTHOR'S CONTRIBUTION TO THE WORK
Anonymous? ☐ Yes ☒ No
Pseudonymous? ☐ Yes ☒ No
If the answer to either of these questions is "Yes," see detailed instructions.

NATURE OF AUTHORSHIP Briefly describe nature of the material created by this author in which copyright is claimed. ▼
Words and music

NOTE
Under the law, the "author" of a "work made for hire" is generally the employer, not the employee (see instructions). For any part of this work that was "made for hire" check "Yes" in the space provided, give the employer (or other person for whom the work was prepared) as "Author" of that part, and leave the space for dates of birth and death blank.

b

NAME OF AUTHOR ▼

DATES OF BIRTH AND DEATH
Year Born ▼   Year Died ▼

Was this contribution to the work a "work made for hire"?
☐ Yes
☐ No

AUTHOR'S NATIONALITY OR DOMICILE
Name of country
OR { Citizen of ▶
Domiciled in ▶

WAS THIS AUTHOR'S CONTRIBUTION TO THE WORK
Anonymous? ☐ Yes ☐ No
Pseudonymous? ☐ Yes ☐ No
If the answer to either of these questions is "Yes," see detailed instructions.

NATURE OF AUTHORSHIP Briefly describe nature of the material created by this author in which copyright is claimed. ▼

c

NAME OF AUTHOR ▼

DATES OF BIRTH AND DEATH
Year Born ▼   Year Died ▼

Was this contribution to the work a "work made for hire"?
☐ Yes
☐ No

AUTHOR'S NATIONALITY OR DOMICILE
Name of Country
OR { Citizen of ▶
Domiciled in ▶

WAS THIS AUTHOR'S CONTRIBUTION TO THE WORK
Anonymous? ☐ Yes ☐ No
Pseudonymous? ☐ Yes ☐ No
If the answer to either of these questions is "Yes," see detailed instructions.

NATURE OF AUTHORSHIP Briefly describe nature of the material created by this author in which copyright is claimed. ▼

3 **YEAR IN WHICH CREATION OF THIS WORK WAS COMPLETED** This information must be given in all cases.
1985 ◀ Year

DATE AND NATION OF FIRST PUBLICATION OF THIS PARTICULAR WORK
Complete this information Month ▶ _____ Day ▶ _____ Year ▶ _____
ONLY if this work has been published. ◀ Nation

4 **COPYRIGHT CLAIMANT(S)** Name and address must be given even if the claimant is the same as the author given in space 2.▼

Simon Glick
1234 Main Street
Southtown, B.C. Canada V1K 2G1

See instructions before completing this space

TRANSFER If the claimant(s) named here in space 4 are different from the author(s) named in space 2, give a brief statement of how the claimant(s) obtained ownership of the copyright.▼

APPLICATION RECEIVED

ONE DEPOSIT RECEIVED

TWO DEPOSITS RECEIVED

REMITTANCE NUMBER AND DATE

DO NOT WRITE HERE OFFICE USE ONLY

MORE ON BACK ▶ • Complete all applicable spaces (numbers 5-9) on the reverse side of this page
• See detailed instructions   • Sign the form at line 8

DO NOT WRITE HERE

Page 1 of _____ pages

SAMPLE #5 — Continued

DO NOT WRITE ABOVE THIS LINE. IF YOU NEED MORE SPACE, USE A SEPARATE CONTINUATION SHEET.

PREVIOUS REGISTRATION Has registration for this work, or for an earlier version of this work, already been made in the Copyright Office?
☐ Yes ☒ No If your answer is "Yes," why is another registration being sought? (Check appropriate box) ▼
☐ This is the first published edition of a work previously registered in unpublished form.
☐ This is the first application submitted by this author as copyright claimant.
☐ This is a changed version of the work, as shown by space 6 on this application.
If your answer is "Yes," give: **Previous Registration Number ▼**   **Year of Registration ▼**

5

DERIVATIVE WORK OR COMPILATION Complete both space 6a & 6b for a derivative work; complete only 6b for a compilation.
a. **Preexisting Material** Identify any preexisting work or works that this work is based on or incorporates. ▼

N/A

b. **Material Added to This Work** Give a brief, general statement of the material that has been added to this work and in which copyright is claimed.▼

N/A

6

See instructions before completing this space.

DEPOSIT ACCOUNT If the registration fee is to be charged to a Deposit Account established in the Copyright Office, give name and number of Account.
Name ▼   **Account Number ▼**

N/A   N/A

7

CORRESPONDENCE Give name and address to which correspondence about this application should be sent. Name/Address/Apt/City/State/Zip ▼

Simon Glick
1234 Main Street
Southtown, B.C.
Canada V1K 2G1

Area Code & Telephone Number ▶ (604) 599-2307

Be sure to give your daytime phone ◀ number

8

CERTIFICATION* I, the undersigned, hereby certify that I am the
Check one ▼
☒ author
☐ other copyright claimant
☐ owner of exclusive right(s)
☐ authorized agent of _____
Name of author or other copyright claimant, or owner of exclusive right(s) ▲

of the work identified in this application and that the statements made
by me in this application are correct to the best of my knowledge.

Typed or printed name and date ▼ If this is a published work, this date must be the same as or later than the date of publication given in space 3.

Simon Glick   date ▶ Nov. 14, 198–

Handwritten signature (X) ▼

Simon Glick

9

MAIL CERTIFICATE TO

Certificate will be mailed in window envelope

Name ▼
Simon Glick

Number/Street/Apartment Number ▼
1234 Main Street

City/State/ZIP ▼
Southtown, B.C. Canada V1K 2G1

Have you:
• Completed all necessary spaces?
• Signed your application in space 8?
• Enclosed check or money order for $10 payable to Register of Copyrights?
• Enclosed your deposit material with the application and fee?
MAIL TO: Register of Copyrights. Library of Congress. Washington. D.C. 20559

SAMPLE #6
COPYRIGHT FORM VA
(U.S.)

FORM VA
UNITED STATES COPYRIGHT OFFICE

REGISTRATION NUMBER

VA   VAU

EFFECTIVE DATE OF REGISTRATION

Month   Day   Year

DO NOT WRITE ABOVE THIS LINE. IF YOU NEED MORE SPACE, USE A SEPARATE CONTINUATION SHEET.

1

TITLE OF THIS WORK ▼
On Top of the World

NATURE OF THIS WORK ▼ See instructions
Album cover

PREVIOUS OR ALTERNATIVE TITLES ▼
N/A

PUBLICATION AS A CONTRIBUTION   If this work was published as a contribution to a periodical, serial, or collection, give information about the collective work in which the contribution appeared.   **Title of Collective Work ▼**

If published in a periodical or serial give: Volume ▼   Number ▼   Issue Date ▼   On Pages ▼

2

NOTE

Under the law. the "author" of a work made for hire' is generally the employer. not the employee (see instructions). For any part of this work that was "made for hire" check "Yes" in the space provided, give the employer (or other person for whom the work was prepared) as "Author" of that part, and leave the space for dates of birth and death blank

a NAME OF AUTHOR ▼
Hortense Smith

DATES OF BIRTH AND DEATH
Year Born ▼ 1948   Year Died ▼

Was this contribution to the work a "work made for hire"?
☐ Yes
☒ No

AUTHOR'S NATIONALITY OR DOMICILE
Name of Country
OR { Citizen of ▶ United States
Domiciled in ▶ United States

WAS THIS AUTHOR'S CONTRIBUTION TO THE WORK
Anonymous? ☒ Yes ☐ No
Pseudonymous? ☐ Yes ☒ No
If the answer to either of these questions is "Yes," see detailed instructions

NATURE OF AUTHORSHIP   Briefly describe nature of the material created by this author in which copyright is claimed. ▼
Album cover concept and design

b NAME OF AUTHOR ▼

DATES OF BIRTH AND DEATH
Year Born ▼   Year Died ▼

Was this contribution to the work a "work made for hire"?
☐ Yes
☐ No

AUTHOR'S NATIONALITY OR DOMICILE
Name of Country
OR { Citizen of ▶
Domiciled in ▶

WAS THIS AUTHOR'S CONTRIBUTION TO THE WORK
Anonymous? ☐ Yes ☐ No
Pseudonymous? ☐ Yes ☐ No
If the answer to either of these questions is "Yes," see detailed instructions.

NATURE OF AUTHORSHIP   Briefly describe nature of the material created by this author in which copyright is claimed. ▼

c NAME OF AUTHOR ▼

DATES OF BIRTH AND DEATH
Year Born ▼   Year Died ▼

Was this contribution to the work a "work made for hire"?
☐ Yes
☐ No

AUTHOR'S NATIONALITY OR DOMICILE
Name of Country
OR { Citizen of ▶
Domiciled in ▶

WAS THIS AUTHOR'S CONTRIBUTION TO THE WORK
Anonymous? ☐ Yes ☐ No
Pseudonymous? ☐ Yes ☐ No
If the answer to either of these questions is. "Yes." see detailed instructions

NATURE OF AUTHORSHIP   Briefly describe nature of the material created by this author in which copyright is claimed. ▼

3

YEAR IN WHICH CREATION OF THIS WORK WAS COMPLETED This information must be given in all cases.
1985 ◄ Year

DATE AND NATION OF FIRST PUBLICATION OF THIS PARTICULAR WORK
Complete this information ONLY if this work has been published.
Month ▶ March   Day ▶ 5   Year ▶ 1985
Canada ◄ Nation

4

See instructions before completing this space

COPYRIGHT CLAIMANT(S) Name and address must be given even if the claimant is the same as the author given in space 2.▼
Hortense Smith
28506 - 115th Ave.
West Dogpatch, Pennsylvania 73205

TRANSFER If the claimant(s) named here in space 4 are different from the author(s) named in space 2, give a brief statement of how the claimant(s) obtained ownership of the copyright.▼

APPLICATION RECEIVED

ONE DEPOSIT RECEIVED

TWO DEPOSITS RECEIVED

REMITTANCE NUMBER AND DATE

DO NOT WRITE HERE OFFICE USE ONLY

MORE ON BACK ▶   • Complete all applicable spaces (numbers 5-9) on the reverse side of this page
   • See detailed instructions.   • Sign the form at line 8

DO NOT WRITE HERE
Page 1 of _____ pages

EXAMINED BY	FORM VA
CHECKED BY	

☐ CORRESPONDENCE Yes

☐ DEPOSIT ACCOUNT FUNDS USED

FOR
COPYRIGHT
OFFICE
USE
ONLY

DO NOT WRITE ABOVE THIS LINE. IF YOU NEED MORE SPACE, USE A SEPARATE CONTINUATION SHEET.

PREVIOUS REGISTRATION Has registration for this work, or for an earlier version of this work, already been made in the Copyright Office?
☐ Yes ☒ No If your answer is "Yes," why is another registration being sought? (Check appropriate box) ▼
☐ This is the first published edition of a work previously registered in unpublished form.
☐ This is the first application submitted by this author as copyright claimant.
☐ This is a changed version of the work, as shown by space 6 on this application.
If your answer is "Yes," give: **Previous Registration Number** ▼   **Year of Registration** ▼

5

DERIVATIVE WORK OR COMPILATION Complete both space 6a & 6b for a derivative work; complete only 6b for a compilation.
a. **Preexisting Material** Identify any preexisting work or works that this work is based on or incorporates. ▼

N/A

b. **Material Added to This Work** Give a brief, general statement of the material that has been added to this work and in which copyright is claimed. ▼

N/A

6

See instructions
before completing
this space

DEPOSIT ACCOUNT If the registration fee is to be charged to a Deposit Account established in the Copyright Office, give name and number of Account.
Name ▼   **Account Number** ▼
N/A   N/A

7

CORRESPONDENCE Give name and address to which correspondence about this application should be sent. Name/Address/Apt/City/State/Zip ▼

Hortense Smith
28506 - 115th Avenue
West Dogpatch, Pennsylvania   73205

Area Code & Telephone Number ▶

Be sure to
give your
daytime phone
◀ number

CERTIFICATION* I, the undersigned, hereby certify that I am the
Check only one ▼
☒ author
[ ] other copyright claimant
[ ] owner of exclusive right(s)
[ ] authorized agent of
                    Name of author or other copyright claimant, or owner of exclusive right(s) ▲

of the work identified in this application and that the statements made
by me in this application are correct to the best of my knowledge.

Typed or printed name and date ▼ If this is a published work, this date must be the same as or later than the date of publication given in space 3.
Hortense Smith   date ▶ May 2, 198-

Handwritten signature (X) ▼   Hortense Smith

8

MAIL CERTIFI-CATE TO

Name ▼
Hortense Smith

Number Street Apartment Number ▼
28506 - 115th Avenue

Certificate will be mailed in window envelope

City State ZIP ▼
West Dogpatch, Pennsylvania   73205

Have you:
• Completed all necessary spaces?
• Signed your application in space 8?
• Enclosed check or money order for $10 payable to Register of Copyrights?
• Enclosed your deposit material with the application and fee?
MAIL TO: Register of Copyrights, Library of Congress, Washington, D.C. 20559

9

* 17 U.S.C. § 506(e) Any person who knowingly makes a false representation of a material fact in the application for copyright registration provided for by section 409, or in any written statement filed in connection with the application, shall be fined not more than $2,500.

☆U.S. GOVERNMENT PRINTING OFFICE: 1981: 355-312

Nov. 1981-600,000

SAMPLE #7
COPYRIGHT FORM TX
(U.S.)

FORM TX
UNITED STATES COPYRIGHT OFFICE

REGISTRATION NUMBER

TX   TXU

EFFECTIVE DATE OF REGISTRATION

Month   Day   Year

DO NOT WRITE ABOVE THIS LINE. IF YOU NEED MORE SPACE, USE A SEPARATE CONTINUATION SHEET.

1

TITLE OF THIS WORK ▼

On Top of the World

PREVIOUS OR ALTERNATIVE TITLES ▼

N/A

PUBLICATION AS A CONTRIBUTION If this work was published as a contribution to a periodical, serial, or collection, give information about the collective work in which the contribution appeared. **Title of Collective Work ▼**

N/A

If published in a periodical or serial give: **Volume ▼**   **Number ▼**   **Issue Date ▼**   **On Pages ▼**

N/A

2

a

NAME OF AUTHOR ▼

Simon Glick

DATES OF BIRTH AND DEATH
Year Born ▼ 1946   Year Died ▼

Was this contribution to the work a "work made for hire"?
☐ Yes
☒ No

AUTHOR'S NATIONALITY OR DOMICILE
Name of Country
OR { Citizen of ▶ Canada
    { Domiciled in ▶ Canada

WAS THIS AUTHOR'S CONTRIBUTION TO THE WORK
Anonymous? ☒ Yes ☐ No
Pseudonymous? ☐ Yes ☒ No
If the answer to either of these questions is "Yes," see detailed instructions.

NATURE OF AUTHORSHIP Briefly describe nature of the material created by this author in which copyright is claimed. ▼
Album liner notes and cover material

NOTE

Under the law, the "author" of a "work made for hire" is generally the employer, not the employee (see instructions). For any part of this work that was "made for hire" check "Yes" in the space provided, give the employer (or other person for whom the work was prepared) as "Author" of that part and leave the space for dates of birth and death blank.

b

NAME OF AUTHOR ▼

DATES OF BIRTH AND DEATH
Year Born ▼   Year Died ▼

Was this contribution to the work a "work made for hire"?
☐ Yes
☐ No

AUTHOR'S NATIONALITY OR DOMICILE
Name of Country
OR { Citizen of ▶
    { Domiciled in ▶

WAS THIS AUTHOR'S CONTRIBUTION TO THE WORK
Anonymous? ☐ Yes ☐ No
Pseudonymous? ☐ Yes ☐ No
If the answer to either of these questions is "Yes," see detailed instructions

NATURE OF AUTHORSHIP Briefly describe nature of the material created by this author in which copyright is claimed. ▼

c

NAME OF AUTHOR ▼

DATES OF BIRTH AND DEATH
Year Born ▼   Year Died ▼

Was this contribution to the work a "work made for hire"?
☐ Yes
☐ No

AUTHOR'S NATIONALITY OR DOMICILE
Name of Country
OR { Citizen of ▶
    { Domiciled in ▶

WAS THIS AUTHOR'S CONTRIBUTION TO THE WORK
Anonymous? ☐ Yes ☐ No
Pseudonymous? ☐ Yes ☐ No
If the answer to either of these questions is "Yes," see detailed instructions

NATURE OF AUTHORSHIP Briefly describe nature of the material created by this author in which copyright is claimed. ▼

3

YEAR IN WHICH CREATION OF THIS WORK WAS COMPLETED This information must be given in all cases.
◀ Year 1985

DATE AND NATION OF FIRST PUBLICATION OF THIS PARTICULAR WORK
Complete this information ONLY if this work has been published.
Month ▶ March   Day ▶ 5   Year ▶ 1985
Canada   ◀ Nation

4

See instructions before completing this space.

COPYRIGHT CLAIMANT(S) Name and address must be given even if the claimant is the same as the author given in space 2. ▼

Simon Glick
1234 Main Street
Southtown, B.C.
Canada   V1K 2G1

TRANSFER If the claimant(s) named here in space 4 are different from the author(s) named in space 2, give a brief statement of how the claimant(s) obtained ownership of the copyright. ▼

APPLICATION RECEIVED

ONE DEPOSIT RECEIVED

TWO DEPOSITS RECEIVED

REMITTANCE NUMBER AND DATE

DO NOT WRITE HERE
OFFICE USE ONLY

MORE ON BACK ▶
• Complete all applicable spaces (numbers 5-11) on the reverse side of this page.
• See detailed instructions.
• Sign the form at line 10.

DO NOT WRITE HERE

Page 1 of _____ pages

133

SAMPLE #7 — Continued

DO NOT WRITE ABOVE THIS LINE. IF YOU NEED MORE SPACE, USE A SEPARATE CONTINUATION SHEET.

PREVIOUS REGISTRATION Has registration for this work, or for an earlier version of this work, already been made in the Copyright Office?
☐ Yes ☐ No If your answer is "Yes," why is another registration being sought? (Check appropriate box) ▼
☐ This is the first published edition of a work previously registered in unpublished form.
☐ This is the first application submitted by this author as copyright claimant.
☐ This is a changed version of the work, as shown by space 6 on this application.
If your answer is "Yes," give: **Previous Registration Number** ▼   **Year of Registration** ▼

5

DERIVATIVE WORK OR COMPILATION Complete both space 6a & 6b for a derivative work; complete only 6b for a compilation.
a. Preexisting Material Identify any preexisting work or works that this work is based on or incorporates. ▼

b. Material Added to This Work Give a brief, general statement of the material that has been added to this work and in which copyright is claimed. ▼

See instructions before completing this space

6

MANUFACTURERS AND LOCATIONS If this is a published work consisting preponderantly of nondramatic literary material in English, the law may require that the copies be manufactured in the United States or Canada for full protection. If so, the names of the manufacturers who performed certain processes, and the places where these processes were performed **must** be given. See instructions for details.
Names of Manufacturers ▼   **Places of Manufacture** ▼

7

REPRODUCTION FOR USE OF BLIND OR PHYSICALLY HANDICAPPED INDIVIDUALS A signature on this form at space 10, and a check in one of the boxes here in space 8, constitutes a non-exclusive grant of permission to the Library of Congress to reproduce and distribute solely for the blind and physically handicapped and under the conditions and limitations prescribed by the regulations of the Copyright Office: (1) copies of the work identified in space 1 of this application in Braille (or similar tactile symbols); or (2) phonorecords embodying a fixation of a reading of that work; or (3) both.
a ☐ Copies and Phonorecords   b ☐ Copies Only   c ☐ Phonorecords Only

See instructions

8

DEPOSIT ACCOUNT If the registration fee is to be charged to a Deposit Account established in the Copyright Office, give name and number of Account.
Name ▼   **Account Number** ▼

9

CORRESPONDENCE Give name and address to which correspondence about this application should be sent. Name/Address/Apt/City/State/Zip ▼

Be sure to give your daytime phone ◀ number

Area Code & Telephone Number ▶

CERTIFICATION* I, the undersigned, hereby certify that I am the
Check one ▶
☐ author
☐ other copyright claimant
☐ owner of exclusive right(s)
☐ authorized agent of _____
of the work identified in this application and that the statements made   Name of author or other copyright claimant, or owner of exclusive right(s) ▲
by me in this application are correct to the best of my knowledge.

Typed or printed name and date ▼ If this is a published work, this date must be the same as or later than the date of publication given in space 3.

_____ date ▶ _____

Handwritten signature (X) ▼

10

MAIL CERTIFICATE TO

Name ▼

Number Street Apartment Number ▼

City State ZIP ▼

Certificate will be mailed in window envelope

Have you:
• Completed all necessary spaces?
• Signed your application in space 10?
• Enclosed check or money order for $10 payable to Register of Copyrights?
• Enclosed your deposit material with the application and fee?
MAIL TO: Register of Copyrights Library of Congress Washington D.C. 20559

11

b. CANADIAN COPYRIGHT REGISTRATION

The Canadian Copyright Act dates back to 1921 and hasn't changed much since that time. To date, the Canadian government has not seen fit to make changes to the act as has occurred in the United States.

1. What can be registered

The Canadian Copyright Act defines a "musical work" as "any combination of melody and harmony, or either of them, printed, reduced to writing, or otherwise graphically produced or reproduced."

There is no provision for registration by way of cassette tape. Cassette tapes weren't even invented when the legislation was written. You can, however, copyright a record or tape in Canada (the act says "records, perforated rolls, and other contrivances by means of which sounds may be mechanically reproduced") as a musical work. A record jacket could be copyrighted as either an "artistic work" or a "literary work."

If you are trying to copyright a song in Canada, you must use a lead sheet or, if you wish, a full arrangement of the song. You cannot use a cassette tape or phonographic record as you can in the United States.

2. Benefits of registration

In Canada, you will receive a Certificate of Registration, when you register your copyright, but not much else.

If you apply for registration of a published work, you must deposit two copies of the work with the National Library of Canada. In the case of an unpublished work, there is no deposit requirement. Deposit requirements vary with the type of work (books or records) and the Canadian content of the material.

By registering your song, you give notification to the copyright office that you own a certain musical work with a certain title. But this copyright system provides very limited evidence. The problem is that the certificate you receive shows the name of the work only, and not its content or form.

In the United States, you send a copy of your work with your registration. In Canada, you do not; only the title is recorded. Thus it is impossible to prove infringement merely by the certificate of copyright. This means that you should follow the steps for "poor man's copyright" in addition to copyright registration (see chapter 13).

The benefits of registration that flow to the copyright owner in the United States are not present in Canada. The certificate only provides a minimal amount of evidence. There is no level of statutory damages nor is there any payment of legal costs. There simply isn't a lot of benefit to registration in Canada.

3. How to apply

Canada uses only two forms for copyright registration. Form 9 is used for a published work; Form 10 is used for an unpublished work. These are simple one-page documents that are very easy to complete. A song would be listed as a "musical" work — after that, you simply add the title and the author's name and address. In the case of published works, you have to add the date and location of initial publication. See Samples #8 and #9.

You can obtain Canadian copyright forms from the copyright office in Ottawa. The address is given in the Appendix.

After completing the form (and making a copy for yourself) mail it, together with $25, to the copyright office. You will receive your certificate in return. That's it. If the work is published all you need to do after that is fulfill the National Library deposit requirement.

It's a very simple process but, unfortunately, it doesn't provide much protection.

4. Registration by tape or record

In Canada, you can register a tape or record but you cannot use a tape or record to register your original songs. You must use a lead sheet or, if you wish, a full arrangement of the song. You can also obtain a copyright certificate for a record album as a literary or artistic work.

SAMPLE #8
COPYRIGHT FORM 9
(Canada)

Consumer and
Corporate Affairs Canada

Consommation
et Corporations Canada

APPLICATION FOR REGISTRATION OF COPYRIGHT IN A PUBLISHED WORK

FORM 9

I, (we) _____ SAMUEL SINGER _____
(Here insert full name and full address of proprietor(s))

_____ 123 MOUNTAIN LANE _____

_____ VANCOUVER, BRITISH COLUMBIA _____

hereby declare that I am(we are) the owner(s) of the Copyright in the original

_____ MUSICAL _____ work
(Here insert: literary, dramatic, musical or artistic, as the case may be)

entitled _____ "MOUNTAIN MOODS" _____
(Here insert title only (no descriptive matter))

by _____ SAMUEL SINGER _____
(Here insert full name and full address of author(s))

_____ 123 MOUNTAIN LANE _____

_____ VANCOUVER, BRITISH COLUMBIA _____
and that the said work was first published by the issue of copies thereof to the public on the

_____ 1st _____ day of _____ May _____ 198– _____
(month)

in the _City of Vancouver_ of _British Columbia, Canada_
(city, town)   (province, state, country)

and I(we) hereby request you to register the Copyright of the said work in my (our) name(s) in accordance

with the provisions of the Copyright Act.

I(We) forward herewith the fee of $25.00 for the examination, registration and issue of a certificate of registration

of copyright.

Dated at _Vancouver_ this _1st_ day of _June_ 198–
(city, town)   (month)

Samuel Singer
Signature(s) (See Rule 33)

The Commissioner of Patent
The Copyright Office,
Ottawa-Hull, Canada
K1A 0C9

CCA-776 (11-81)

Canada

137

SAMPLE #9
COPYRIGHT FORM 10
(Canada)

Consumer and
Corporate Affairs Canada

Consommation
et Corporations Canada

APPLICATION FOR REGISTRATION OF COPYRIGHT   IN AN UNPUBLISHED WORK

FORM 10

I, (we) _____ SAMUEL SINGER _____
(Here insert full name and full address of proprietor(s))

_____ 123 MOUNTAIN LANE _____

_____ VANCOUVER, BRITISH COLUMBIA _____

hereby declare that I am(we are) the owner(s) of the Copyright in the original

_____ MUSICAL _____ work
(Here insert: literary, dramatic, musical or artistic, as the case may be)

entitled _____ "MOUNTAIN MOODS" _____
(Here insert title only (no descriptive matter).

_____

by _____ SAMUEL SINGER _____
(Here insert full name and full address of author(s))

_____ 123 MOUNTAIN LANE _____

_____ VANCOUVER, BRITISH COLUMBIA _____
and that the said work has not been published and I(we) hereby request you to register the Copyright of

the said work in my(our) name(s), in accordance with the provisions of the Copyright Act.

I(We) forward herewith the fee of $25.00 for the examination, registration and issue of a certificate of re-

gistration of copyright.

Dated at _____ Vancouver _____ this _____ 1st _____ day of _____ June _____ 19 ___ 8–
(city, town)   (month)

Samuel Singer
(Signature(s) (See Rule 3))

The Commissioner of Patents,
The Copyright Office,
Ottawa - Hull, Canada
K1A 0C9

CCA-775 (11-81)

Canadä

138

As the definition of musical works contains the provision that such works have to be "reduced to writing or otherwise graphically produced or reproduced," chances are a tape sent to yourself would secure poor man's copyright but would not satisfy the requirements of registration under the Copyright Act.

5. Duration and public domain

In Canada, copyright lasts for your own life plus a further 50 years. As in the United States, in the case of two or more songwriters, the 50-year period commences with the death of the last survivor. In the case of mechanical contrivances, such as records, the copyright period is 50 years from the date of the master recording.

6. Transfer

Transfers, or assignments of the copyright, must be in writing and signed by the person transferring the rights. An assignment or transfer may be registered and, for safety's sake, should be. This is done by submitting the original transfer together with a certified copy to the copyright office. The copyright office stamps the original and returns it; the certified copy of the transfer is kept on file.

There is a time limitation for transfers in Canada. Any transfer may be voluntarily limited as to duration by the parties who initially agree to it. The maximum limit is the life of the author plus 25 years. As copyright lasts for the life of the author plus 50 years, the remaining 25 years of the copyright term goes to the heirs.

A somewhat quaint provision is that even after an assignment, the author has the right to claim authorship as well as a separate right "to restrain any distortion, mutilation, or other modification of the work that would be prejudicial to his honour or reputation."

7. A final word to Canadian songwriters

The Canadian Copyright Act which does not require a deposit of your song, is simply not very effective in providing protection. If you proceed with registration in Canada, follow the common law or poor man's copyright procedures outlined in chapter 13. You should do this to fix not only the title of your material but its content as well.

After you get back the certificate from the copyright office, you should attach a copy of your material to the certificate and file these away in a safe place. As well, send a copy of your material by registered letter to yourself, your lawyer, or SRS, (or other similar bodies in the United States). This ties the material to the title you have registered. Remember, you might have to register twice — once for an unpublished work and the second time for a published work.

15

PUBLISHERS

If you are writing your own material, you need to look for a music publisher. The word publisher is rather a misnomer. In today's music business, a better term would be music promoter.

Around the turn of the century, a music publisher was the person who took your song, printed it, and sold the sheet music. If you were lucky and the song was a hit, the publisher might also prepare the perforated rolls necessary for player pianos. Beyond these basics, promotion was a strong aspect of a music publisher's business. The publisher would try to interest other people in performing your music in order to obtain performing rights from performers and increase sales of sheet music. The more people the publisher could interest, the more copies of sheet music would be produced and sold. This meant more money for the publisher and more money for you.

Sheet music doesn't account for much these days and perforated rolls are found in antique shops. The role of music publisher as a promoter and copyright administrator has increased by leaps and bounds. This development mirrors the changing face of the music business and the new technology that forms a part of it.

a. SELECTING A PUBLISHER

You can find a publisher in much the same fashion as you find an agent, manager, or other personal representative. Ask other songwriters for recommendations, and check in books like *Songwriter's Market* (Writer's Digest Books, Ohio). Circulate your promo kit together with demo tapes of your material. If contacted by a publisher, check out the credibility. Which songwriters does the publisher act for? How successful are they? Which performers does the publisher have contact with?

Some publishers specialize in certain types of music. If the publisher who contacts you specializes in your type of music, that's just great. If, however, he is into country and western and you are into Top 40, you are looking at the wrong publisher.

You want a publisher who is active in your type of music, has contacts with known performers and record companies, who has a demonstrated track record, and who is a person you can work with on a long-term basis.

The industry recognizes two types of publishers. The first are publishing companies that are direct affiliates or branches of record companies. Columbia Records, for example, has its own publishing division known as Chappell Music Co. This type of publisher has stature within the industry. The second type are independent publishers. These are not affiliated with any particular record company, although they may have connections. Until a few years ago, independents were almost unknown; now, they abound.

b. PUBLISHERS AND PERFORMING RIGHTS

You and your publisher *must* belong to the same performing rights organization. Because of this, most publishers have two or three companies. One company would be a publisher member of ASCAP, the second of BMI; in Canada, it would be CAPCAN and PROCAN. If you have not yet made a decision as to which of the performing rights organizations to join, your choice of publisher may be a factor in your selection. Your publisher may also be able to provide reasons to help you decide.

Performing rights organizations split the money they receive among themselves, the publisher, and the songwriter. Usually, they take a 4% commission for themselves, and pay out not less than 50% to the songwriter.

For more on performing rights societies, see chapter 16.

c. THE CONTRACT

As you might expect, music publishers tend to have their own standard form contracts. Before you sign any contract with a music publisher, check it over with your lawyer. This is a long-term relationship, and you hope, a successful one. You have to be comfortable with the relationship and understand what it includes.

Your contract with your music publisher will have certain basic elements. It will, for example, transfer all rights in the copyright of your material to the publisher. In exchange for the transfer of rights, the publisher agrees to pay you a percentage of the money received. You should expect 50% of all earnings from the performing rights, which will be paid out to you directly by the performing rights organization, not through your publisher. The percentage from mechanical rights may be the same or slightly different. Foreign rights, both of performing and mechanical rights, will have a lesser percentage. Publication of sheet music will provide yet another rate. Although it would be easier to specify 50% of everything received, most publisher/songwriter agreements break up the rights into different categories and different percentages. Check with your lawyer and with other songwriters to determine what the going rates are.

The contract will have a set term (normally three to five years) and may provide for termination if either party is unhappy with the relationship. Arbitration is also a standard provision. You should have the right, as well, to check the publisher's books of account to make sure all the figures tally up, and to cancel the agreement under certain circumstances.

The importance of this contract cannot be overstated. Remember, you are transferring to the publisher all the rights in your song for a certain term. This may include songs you have written in the past (prior to finding a publisher), as well as all songs written during the time of your contract. As you have assigned all copyright, you have to be sure that the other parts of the agreement provide you with adequate compensation for your work.

A very important provision in any agreement between a songwriter and music publisher is the reversion at the end of the term of the agreement. Do you have to buy these rights back? Do the publisher's rights to any particular song terminate if it has not been a successful seller within a specified time span? Options for further works are also part of the normal contract. Review all of these terms with your lawyer.

d. THE SONGWRITERS' GUILD

It isn't a union, it's a guild. But dollar for dollar, you can't get a better deal.

Under different names, the Guild has been around since 1931. Over the years, it has prepared a number of standard form agreements for use by publishers and songwriters. All have been fair. Write to the Guild at the address given in the Appendix to get membership forms and an information kit.

As a member, you get copies of the Guild's recommended songwriters' agreement. In addition, the Guild will review any contract you get, and will recommend changes or additions or give you advice on percentages. It will collect your royalties, find a collaborator, and will audit your publisher. It will appraise catalogues of songs to determine their value, and will file termination notices for you. Other benefits of membership include access to a group medical and life insurance policy. For a songwriter, it's a bargain.

e. MUSIC PUBLISHERS AND PROMOTION

A good music publisher will have a variety of contacts with record companies, performers, and just about everybody in the music business. The object of the exercise is to circulate your song among these people in an attempt to get a major recording artist to perform and record your song. Most publishers are extremely cagey about this side of the business. If they have a contact, they don't want to abuse it. If they don't think your song is appropriate for a particular performer, even if you do, the publisher will not damage his or her credibility with the performer by sending the music on. The publisher, in effect, targets the performer for your music by fitting the two together.

A publisher may well try to adopt your song to a slightly different market. For example, a Top 40 or a middle-of-the-road song may well become a country and western ballad. Cross-over songs, as they are known, can be extremely good money-makers. As your publisher is, or should be, knowledgeable about the music business and about what is or is not saleable, listen to any helpful comments. Maybe slight modifications to your material will produce a hit.

To further interest people in your song, the publisher may also prepare a demo. If this is done, it is normally done on a professional basis. Your publisher hires a group (perhaps even yours) and pays for a professional recording studio to prepare the demo. Your publisher will then send the demo to performers who might be interested in the material.

Your contract should specify who pays for this demo record. The publisher should absorb this cost; be very cautious if this is not the case. You may pay out a lot of money for no reward.

A reputable music publisher will take on the costs of recording your demo. You will not be charged for this or other services. A publisher's income comes from the revenues generated by the song and not by defrauding songwriters.

f. ADMINISTRATION OF THE ROYALTIES

The primary job of your publisher is to get your song recorded by a well known artist. The second job is to collect money from this recording and to account to you for such money. Your publisher should be on top of all royalties, should know when they are in arrears, and should follow up on any problems. A publisher's books and records should be sufficient to show which groups have acquired rights and are paying royalties for your song, when these royalties are due, and what royalties of each type on each have been received. If a publisher is not satisfied with the credits awarded by a performing rights organization, he or she should go to bat on your behalf. A good publisher will follow through on all royalty aspects of your song to increase the income for both of you.

g. SO YOU WANT TO BE YOUR OWN PUBLISHER

You may consider publishing your song by yourself. After all, you would get 100% of the royalties rather than 50%. But sometimes you have to spend money to make money.

A good publisher is invaluable. A publisher's talents and yours should be complementary. Chances are, if you are a successful songwriter, you would not be a successful publisher. The skills involved in both jobs take too much time to be good at both. Nonetheless, many songwriters wish to be their own publishers and, for some, it works.

Look over the promotional and administrative functions of a publisher. Are you prepared to do these things? Do you have the skills necessary to do them? Are you well enough known? If you are, great. If not, look for a publisher.

There is, however, an intermediate step that tries to give you the benefit of both worlds. It's not totally successful, but it can work.

Let's say your band incorporates. The copyright of a particular song is owned by one or two members and not the band itself. They enter into a songwriter/publisher agreement with the company, which is the band. The band's company, in turn, enters into a publishing agreement with a recognized independent or affiliated publisher. With luck, and depending upon negotiation, the band would then receive 25% of any profits, the recognized publisher 25%, and the two songwriters would share 50%. They, of course, would also share in the band's 25%. You can vary this formula however you wish.

146

Under this arrangement, the band, as a company, would share the cost of the demo with the record publisher, and the band would probably record the demo. It can be a good working relationship. If you go this route, remember that your publishing company should be a member of the performing rights organization. You may, as well, need an affiliate publishing company to cover the other performing rights organizations.

A songwriter who is extremely successful may form a publishing company in which both a major publishing company and the songwriter are shareholders. Percentages will be divided according to skill.

Some people turn to this route in desperation. If they have been unable to obtain a contract with a publisher, the development of their own company is the only route left. However, don't consider this route until you are very well known in the music business. It is an expensive alternative. Not only do you have the cost of forming the company, you must pay the cost of all demo records as well. You must also have the time to promote and administer the copyright for your songs.

Aside from performing rights, your own company should also be affiliated with the Harry Fox Agency or another mechanical rights organization (see chapter 17).

Many well known performers have their own publishing companies. As a general rule, these publishing companies then become associated with another publishing company. It is not unknown for a major entertainer to demand the publishing rights to any song recorded. As with most aspects of the music business, the degree of negotiation depends upon the stature of the performer or songwriter.

16

PERFORMING RIGHTS SOCIETIES

One of the rights you obtain when you copyright your song is the right to perform your work in public — the performing right. It is the right to perform the song in public, over radio and television, in bars and lounges, and anywhere else.

The performing right is part of the bundle of rights associated with copyright, and one of the most lucrative. Because policing or controlling of this right would be difficult, if not impossible, to do by yourself, the performing rights organization does it for you. It does so by licensing every performance of your material — from concerts, to nightclubs, to taverns and bars, to AM and FM radio, and to television. Regardless of whether you are Top 40, disco, country and western, or middle-of-the-road, the same rules apply.

Note that the performing right does not include records, cassettes, or other rights which you had when you copyrighted your material, nor is the performing right paid to a performer of the material, unless he or she also wrote the song. Some of these rights are covered in the next chapter on mechanical rights.

In this chapter, we're going to look at how songwriters get the money from their performing right, and at the performing rights organizations which were set up to protect them.

a. HISTORY

As legend has it, Victor Herbert, a famous songwriter of Tin Pan Alley days, was once dining in a New York hotel. The orchestra on stage was playing some of his songs when he was asked to pay the bill for his meal. Herbert told the hotel that if they paid him for the use of his music, he would pay for the meal.

Later, Herbert and John Philip Sousa, who wrote a number of famous marches and other melodies, got together and formed an association known as The American Society of Composers, Authors, and Publishers, now commonly referred to as ASCAP, to collect royalties from users of music on behalf of songwriters.

Before that famous incident, other well known American composers had died in obscurity and poverty. Steven Foster is the example most often cited in this regard. His *Camptown Races* was and still is a very popular song. Despite its popularity, the only money that Foster received for the song was the initial payment made by his publisher, which wasn't much and certainly not enough. Foster died a pauper.

The copyright laws have given songwriters the sole legal ability to perform their material in public. Herbert and Sousa used this aspect of the law, together with the concept of a performing rights organization borrowed from England, to enforce the collection of royalties from the people who used music for commercial purposes. ASCAP was the first such organization in North America and it quickly became very powerful.

To explain what ASCAP did, one has to look at the way music and the business of music were developing at the time. Around the turn of the century, a songwriter received royalties only from the sale of sheet music or perforated rolls for player pianos, or with luck, by selling a song to a vaudeville performer. But with the technological innovations of the twentieth century, the business of music rapidly became more complex. Recording and other devices were invented that enabled people to listen to music in their own homes, and more live music was being presented to audiences. It became obvious that music had a value. For publishers and composers, it was necessary to develop a *method* for collecting money from the distribution of their songs.

Herbert and Sousa, together with over 200 other composers, banded together with ASCAP. They let it be known that no one would be permitted to play their material in public without payment of a license fee for use of the performing right of the songwriter's copyright. This included live performances and radio performances. They threatened to sue anyone who didn't pay — and sue they did.

Soon, the live entertainment business and the radio stations fell into line. They started to pay a fee for the use of music. At first, payment was made each time a particular piece of music was used. This was given directly to the composer and the publisher of the music. However, the sheer volume of music being used and the difficulty in keeping track of it made an actual count next to impossible. Therefore, a new method had to be selected.

Each restaurant, nightclub, or radio station that used or broadcast music was required to pay an annual fee. The amount of this fee depended upon the number of seats in the club or restaurant, or the number of listeners that the radio station had. Later, the gross income of these establishments was used as the measuring stick for fees. This is still one way of applying a fee measure today.

The effective monopoly of ASCAP was broken by Broadcast Music Incorporated, known as BMI, in 1939. A group of broadcasters rebelled against rate increases imposed by ASCAP, and went on strike. For a time, they broadcast only public domain material and, therefore, were not subject to any actions by ASCAP. These broadcasters formed the second performing rights organization in the United States. BMI now has more member writers and publishers than ASCAP does.

The third and smallest performing rights organization in the United States is known as SESAC, Inc. Like BMI, it is a company and not an association. It is also much smaller than the other two performing rights organizations.

b. CANADIAN PERFORMING RIGHTS ASSOCIATIONS

The development of performing rights organizations in Canada parallels the development in the United States. The Composers, Authors and Publishers Association of Canada Ltd., known as CAPAC, was formed in 1925 (under the name The Canadian Performing Rights Society). It was, at that time, a joint venture of an English society (The Performing Rights Society) and ASCAP. Historically, both organizations and the music of both the United States and England had an impact on Canada. It was only natural that the two performing rights societies would want some base in Canada. However, the market was too small for Canada, so the two organizations co-operated.

PROCAN (The Performing Rights Organization of Canada Ltd.) was founded shortly after BMI in the United States as an offshoot of BMI. At that time it was known as BMI Canada.

Both performing rights organizations in Canada achieved independence from their parents at a later date. CAPAC and PROCAN remain the only two performing rights organizations in Canada.

c. WHAT PERFORMING RIGHTS ORGANIZATIONS DO

Simply put, performing rights organizations exist in order to catalogue the music of the composers they represent and to license others to perform this music in public or broadcast it over radio or television. They charge and collect fees from every radio station, television station, and licensed cabaret, club, or nightspot that uses live entertainment. After collecting this money, the performing rights group then divides it among its member composers and publishers.

Today, performing rights organizations collect a lot of money. Most songwriters and music publishers derive a major portion of their incomes — even over and above record sales — from this source. Your band will not share in this income unless it provides original material. The performing rights societies do not act for the benefit of record companies or performers. Only songwriters or publishing companies need apply.

Any establishment that uses music is required to pay a fee to the performing rights organizations. In both the United States and Canada, most users of music (including taverns, clubs, radio, and television) will pay a fee to all performing rights organizations in their country. This fee is based on the gross income of the business being licensed. Each year, the performing rights organizations review the books and accounts for music users and establish the fee. Ratings of radio and television stations are used also. After allowing for certain specified expenses, the fees come off the top.

Most clubs, as well as radio stations, like paying these fees as much as they like income tax. But it is a necessary evil; if they don't pay, they are not allowed to use the music.

d. HOW THE MONEY GETS DIVIDED

Let's say you write a song or two. It gets published and you join one of the performing rights organizations. How do you get your money?

Let's use radio as an example. Every year, each radio station licensed by a performing rights organization is "sampled." The way in which this sampling is done varies from organization to organization. There is great and heated debate among composers, publishers, and the organizations themselves as to how this sampling should be conducted. Logs may be kept by a radio station and the performing rights organization of all music used. This information forms a bank of statistical data which is later fed into the computers of the performing rights organization. What comes out is a very large formula. They take the total amount of income received by the organization, subtract its costs of operation, and divide the rest by the number of songs being used after factoring in the frequency of each song. One play equals one point. A hit will be played often, hence, earning more points. The money paid is based on the number of points.

e. JOINING A PERFORMING RIGHTS ORGANIZATION

As noted earlier, performing rights organizations exist to assist songwriters and composers. They do not exist for performers. Only if your group, or members of it, start to write songs will you receive the benefits of these organizations. But, you will probably try to work original material into your act as soon as possible. As a composer or a songwriter, you can only join one of the organizations in your own country. Your publisher must be a member of the same performing rights organization.

All of the organizations have some plusses and some minuses. Some songwriters prefer ASCAP simply because of its age and its existence as a society, not a company. Others point out that BMI has been more aggressive, as indicated by its larger membership in a shorter span of time. Because of the monopoly-like aspects to both organizations, ASCAP and BMI are subject to certain court orders in the United States dating from 1941. These orders regulate the operation of both organizations and the rates they charge music users. These orders also make it much easier to join either organization than it had been before.

After you have published one or two songs, you are ready to join. Write to both groups explaining your interest. (Their addresses are listed in the Appendix.) Talk to other songwriters in your area and find out which organization they favor and why. Have your lawyer review each membership agreement you receive and listen to any advice. Each organization has its own standard membership agreement, and there are differences from agreement to agreement. These differences, and the different methods the organizations have of collecting and dividing income, should help you decide which organization is best for you.

The money from any song is normally divided equally between the publishing company and the songwriter. If you set up your own publishing company and it, in turn, joins the same performing rights organization, you will receive 100% of this income. This may sound good, but before you try it, review the preceding chapter on music publishers.

Once you have joined a performing rights organization, you are in for five years. As a rule, this is automatically extended at the end of the term. You can resign, but only on written notice to the performing rights organization. Each organization has slightly different rules regarding termination. Check with your lawyer on the correct procedures to be followed if you wish to terminate your membership.

17

MECHANICAL RIGHTS

a. WHAT ARE MECHANICAL RIGHTS?

When you copyright a song, you obtain the right to license its use for recording and to receive an income from record companies. The right to reproduce a song by way of records, tapes, and other media is called the mechanical right. It is the part of the copyright bundle that gives the songwriter the sole right to reproduce a song in a mechanical fashion.

If another person wants to record your song, he or she must get a compulsory license. This means the other person has the right to make a recording of your music, but has to pay you for doing so. You cannot prevent the other person from making the record, but you can collect a specified royalty for the records made.

This mechanical right, in monetary terms, is quite small. Indeed, most composers think it is too small. In Canada, the rates were established in 1921 and haven't changed since. In the U.S. the rates have increased but are still fairly low.

The compulsory license requires that a firm that wishes to record your music has to pay you the statutory rate — around 3¢ — for each record on which your song appears. The Copyright Act in both countries sets out the statutory or fixed license fee, which is reviewed by the government from time to time.

The act also provides that a person who wishes to use your music can do so by serving you with a notice. This notice must be in a specific form; the acts set out a rather complex procedure of how this form comes to your attention and how you must respond to it. Unfortunately, the complexity makes it too awkward to use on a day-to-day basis. The act also provides for accounting periods and other miscellaneous ways of keeping track of the copies made. This procedure may have worked back in 1921, but is no longer very effective.

b. HARRY FOX AND HIS FRIENDS

Recording companies found the compulsory license a good idea but the procedure too complex to follow. To get around this difficulty, a new organization was formed to take care of mechanical rights by following the voluntary procedure outlined in the Copyright Act instead of the compulsory statutory route. This organization was the Harry Fox Agency, Inc.

The Harry Fox Agency initially served both the United States and Canada. In 1976, the Canadian functions were taken on by the Canadian Musical Reproduction Rights Agency Limited (CMRRA). These agencies administer mechanical rights on behalf of their members, who are publishers — not composers, not songwriters, and not bands. Each publisher will have a contract with its songwriters, which will set out how the mechanical rights fees are to be divided.

In the last several decades, other organizations have sprung up to administer mechanical rights. They also license foreign mechanical rights. These groups are listed in the Appendix.

c. HOW THEY WORK

Let's say you have been asked to do a record. Of the songs on the record, two are "covers," that is, your own versions of songs written by others. How do you get the rights to use someone else's song?

You can follow the compulsory license provisions of the copyright laws, but that can be complicated. Instead, your record producer can contact the mechanical rights companies, as one of them will have the rights to the music you want to use.

In simple terms, your producer or record company will enter into an agreement that requires certain payments. These payments are made by the record company to the mechanical rights group. The mechanical rights group deducts its commission (about 4%) and forwards the balance to the publisher of the song who, in turn, divides the money received, keeping a portion, and sends the rest on to the songwriter.

The same principle applies to records, tapes, and other mechanical ways of reproducing your song. Synchronization rights, for films and videos, are slightly different, but the principle is the same. If a film producer wishes to use your music in a film, you will be paid according to how much of the tune is used, and the use to which it is put.

Mechanical rights have originated from substantial changes in technology. The record player, tape deck, and video machine were unknown until a short time ago. No doubt we will soon be confronted with new developments and new ways for songwriters to make money from mechanical rights in their material.

18

RECORDING

Recording can be a tremendous experience for your band. Your earliest recording will probably be made just to play back your sound to yourself, and to make demo tapes for your promo kit. Later, you may consider cutting a record and signing a recording contract. Of the thousands of bands started every year, only a few get to record. Some just don't want to. Many bands are quite happy playing regular dates in their own area, and travelling a bit. For other bands, the possibility of the big time is the only thing that keeps them going.

a. YOUR FIRST DEMO

Demos, or promotional tapes or recordings, are used a lot in the music business. One will form part of your promo kit for circulation to potential employers, agents, or managers. If you are a songwriter, you may well circulate a demo to potential music publishers, agents, or record companies.

Demos take various forms. During the initial stages of your band, your demos will probably be recorded by you, or by a friend, during one of your rehearsals. Chances are you would probably do this anyway simply to find out how the band sounds. In all likelihood, your first tapes will be done on a home tape recorder with one or two tracks. Compared to the 32-track machine in a recording studio, this may sound like small potatoes. But bear in mind that most records prior to 1965 were recorded on one or two tracks at most. The multi-track machines came much later.

The function of your demos is to encourage people to employ your band, or to get an agent or manager interested. Because they are circulated to potential employers, these tapes are not published. Nonetheless, it makes good sense to protect your band by inserting a copyright notice on every tape you record. The notice should be placed on the tape itself, not on the container. (See chapter 13 for more on copyright notices.)

In the United States, an example of the appropriate notation is:

℗1985, Randy Miller and John Howard
All Rights Reserved

The ℗ notice (for "performing rights") is used on recordings in the same fashion as the © on other materials. This notice should appear on both sides of the tape. In the example above, two names of the band members have been used on the assumption that they own all copyright in the sound recording. If your band is incorporated, you may wish to use the name of the company. Once again, the expression "All Rights Reserved" provides certain additional protection in the United States and other countries.

In Canada, the notice should read:

© 1985, Randy Miller and John Howard

Make sure that this notice appears on both sides of the tape that you send out. That way, you have at least some protection if someone later pirates the material. No one is supposed to use this material for broadcast or other purposes. However, it has been known to happen. Some of the initial Buddy Holly material, submitted by him on demos, was used over the air by certain radio stations in the United States.

Keep track of where your demos have gone. If you are preparing 10 tapes, keep a file on these tapes. List whom they were sent to, when, and if they have been returned (if a return has been requested). This way you know who has the tapes and, at any point in time, where they should be. This tape register should be kept in a safe place as part of the band's books and records.

Chances are these initial tapes of yours will contain no original material. Rather, all songs on the tapes will be cover versions of other performer's materials. As such, the only copyright protection you have is for the tape itself.

b. ORIGINAL MATERIAL

At some time or other, every successful band starts to produce original material. A demo with your original material can well be circulated to music publishers and others with a view to interesting them in your work.

Different publishers have different expectations of what a demo tape should contain. You should check with the current *Songwriter's Market* (Writer's Digest Books), or other publications, to determine the needs and wants of record publishers and others. Some want long tapes; others want no more than four of your best songs. It pays to try and find out what a publisher wants before you submit your material. After all, you want to make a favorable impression and most publishers are pleased that you have shown enough interest to pinpoint what they want.

In your accompanying letter you can provide a list of the songs and indicate, of course, that all are copyrighted. Once again, it is desirable to keep a list of all tapes sent out. If you want a return of these tapes, you normally have to say so in your submission and include a self-addressed stamped envelope for their return.

As with the initial tapes made for your promo kit, demo tapes submitted to a music publisher are not large, expensive productions. They are normally recorded at home or in some other convenient location. In this fashion, your costs can be kept down.

c. STUDIO RECORDING

In time, you will require the services of a recording studio. Home tape recorders are great and can be quite useful. But a 24 or 32-track machine in a professional studio can add a lot to your material.

1. Shop around

Before you decide on which studio to use, check them all out. Ask each for a list of the equipment they have. Visit all of them and look around the facilities. More importantly, talk to other groups who have used the studios and get their comments on the quality of the studio and, if included, the abilities of the engineer and resident producer.

The next step is to make arrangements directly with a studio for the rental of their facility. Studios normally rent out by the hour. This hour may or may not include the services of their engineer, other technicians, and the other facilities of the studio. Find out precisely what is included in the hourly figure. Does it include a professional engineer? Does it include accommodation, refreshments, and other items? Will you be billed extra for the coffee supply? What about additional equipment? Is there an additional charge for using some of the studio's equipment on top of the basic hourly rate?

Review all of these items directly with the studio manager. If anything seems a little uncertain, try to get a written list of what is and is not included. For those items not included, get the additional price on an hourly or other basis.

Because it takes you a while to get the band set up, you should find out whether or not setup time is included in the hourly rate charged by the studio. If you go overtime, some studios may penalize you as they have others waiting to use the facilities. Is there an additional charge of this type and, if so, what is it?

2. The rental agreement

The basic document for the rental of a recording studio is called simply a rental agreement. Many studios have standard forms prepared, which you should review and understand before signing. After all, you will be liable for all the costs you incur while at the studio. If the studio does not have a rental agreement, write down what has been agreed to. Put this in the form of a letter to the studio setting our your understanding of the rental agreements — what is and is not included. If the identity of the engineer is important to you, make sure that you include this in your own letter or that it is included in the rental agreement. Other than that, the standard items such as the time the studio is available for use, the dates on which the studio will be used, and the money you will have to pay for using the studio, should also be included.

There should also be some description of the final product. What do you expect to receive after you leave the studio? Who will be responsible for any mixing? Will the end product be on tape (and what type and speed of tape), or in the form of an acetate or actual phonograph record? Does the studio have the personnel to carry out these functions or will you have to provide additional people to do this work?

As you might expect, you will also be liable for any damage caused to the recording studio by members of the band. If the frustration of a bad recording session ends up with damage to the walls, ceiling, and equipment, the band will be responsible. For this reason it pays to limit the number of people who will be present; your friends should certainly not come to watch.

Some items not normally included in an agreement with the recording studio may be necessary. For example, some recording studios like to be credited and will require this as part of the recording agreement. Others will give you a lower rate for recording if you use the facilities after regular hours. Still others will allow you some time to pay. If there are any unusual payment arrangements, make sure these are set out in black and white. Be wary of giving away a percentage in exchange for studio time. A recording session, for a demo in particular, is not worth 10% of your gross earnings over the next five years!

Try to get the best deal possible for facilities and equipment. Document the agreement between you and the recording studio. The end product, the demo, should be *your* property. However, a recording studio is entitled to hold back on the final product until they have been paid in full, unless alternate payment arrangements have been made. If you need the demo in a hurry for a hot lead, make sure of the payment terms before you go through with the deal.

d. A RECORDING CONTRACT

The goal of many bands is to make a record and to have that record sell "platinum." Of the thousands of records produced every year, only a few reach this end goal.

In many instances, a recording contract might be the worst move your band could make. Your band might not be ready for a recording contract. With many groups, it takes time for the sound to meld together and for the musicians to work as a unit instead of a collection of solo acts. A group that comes together quite quickly, records, and flops is in a worse position than a band that works steadily to develop its own sound until it is ready to make a record. Aside from artistic considerations, a band that has worked together for some time is better prepared in a business sense to enter into a recording contract.

A good manager will not let a group record before its time. A good manager will also help you sort out contract considerations.

1. The basic terms of a recording contract

Making a record is a gamble. A record company is gambling a lot of money in recording costs, promotion costs, and other expenses in the hope that the record will be a hit; the group is gambling its reputation.

As an incentive to the group, the record company will normally provide an advance. This advance may be quite high in the case of a well known performer, or relatively small for a new unknown group. The size of the advance is totally negotiable. If the record company has a lot of faith in the new group, the advance may be quite large. This advance is basically offered as an incentive to sign with one company or another. The payment to the group is called an advance because the record company later recoups this amount out of the royalties otherwise payable to the performers. If the advance is $10,000, the royalties payable to the group (after other deductions) must pay back this $10,000 before any additional money is paid out. Only in rare instances is the initial advance non-recoupable.

In addition to the advance, the record company will pay all production costs including the costs of the record producer, the studio, and all other expenses necessary for the production of a master. Once again, the payment of production costs is viewed as an advance against the performer's royalties. As a result, the record will have to sell sufficient copies for the performer's royalties to cover the full cost of production as well as the initial advance to the performer. This money must be paid back to the record company before the band will see any additional income. In addition to the advance, the band now has to recoup the production cost. And the production costs will probably be at least $50,000.

The production costs to be repaid include all the costs of producing a master. This master is what is used to reproduce records and tapes. These production costs include the cost of any sidemen, the fairly large expense of a producer (who is normally chosen by the record company and not by the band), studio rental fees, equipment rentals, and everything else.

If these expenses are recouped out of the performer's royalty, what does the record company pay for? It should pay for the cost of manufacturing the records and tapes and the cost of promotion and other sales-related expenses. The record company will, of course, have its own overhead (offices, staff, etc.), which it pays out of its portion of the money.

One other rather peculiar aspect of recording contracts is that you become an employee of the record company. This means that part of the production cost will be your own salaries (at scale) for the time spent in recording. This base scale wage, together with the advance, is all you see until the royalties have recouped the other expenses referred to earlier. Your employee status will be documented in the recording contract.

The justification for this is that the record company must have copyright to the master. It's rather like the contract between you and the publisher where your publisher has the copyright to your song. In the same fashion, you will receive a royalty at a specific percentage from the record company (as owner of the copyright to the sound recording).

Major performers are in a position to buy back the master after certain expenses or target profits have been made. Other performers buy back these masters from the record companies when they have become successful. These masters can have quite a high residual value. In your initial recording contracts, you probably won't have too much say in this area, but it is something to think about.

As with advances, percentages can vary considerably. Either the wholesale or retail cost of the record can be used as a starting point. Normally, the packaging costs are deducted before calculating a percentage. The percentage is then calculated on the number of records actually sold. There is a deduction made for returns (normally about 10% of the total royalties). Exclusions are also quite common and must be watched carefully. For example, records given out as "freebies" by a record company, or more particularly a record club, will not generate a royalty. Records given away by the record company in a promotional gimmick will not have a royalty. The list is quite a long one and should be examined closely by you and your lawyer.

The record company chooses the material to be recorded; this is normally done with the consent of the artist. It is usually a three-way street between the record company, the record producer, and the band. From the band's point of view, it is best to include as many of their own as possible as they will then receive the performing and mechanical royalties on these songs.

If a single is made from one song on the album, the flip side should be one of the band's own original songs to take advantage of the additional royalty involved. The more cover material you use, the less royalties will accrue to the members of the band themselves.

Another basic contract consideration is who the parties to the contract will be. Record companies know that bands change their personnel from time to time. Therefore, they will try to get a contract not only with the band as a unit, but the individual performers in it. There are arguments both pro and con to this position. As a solo performer, would you want the same record company? Carefully consider whether or not your solo career (after the band) would be handled well by the same recording company.

A number of other points are covered in a recording contract. Your band will have to be available for publicity of the album, waive certain rights of privacy, and a host of other things. Your record company may well assist in the cost of a new tour in order to promote the album. With these and other considerations, you can see why a knowledgeable manager, lawyer, and accountant should be holding your hand when you sign any recording contract.

2. Cross-collateralization and options

"Cross-collateralization" is an interesting device used by recording companies to recoup their expenses. This can occur in a number of ways. Let's say the first record you make doesn't recoup all the production costs. This doesn't mean the record has not made a profit for the recording company. It simply means that the royalties payable to you have not equalled production costs. Under cross-collateralization the balance owed on the production cost for your first record can be added to the production cost of your second and recouped out of the second record. If your second record is a hit, you might find yourself still repaying the expenses of the first record. Given the costs involved, you generally need a consistent series of winners to recoup all of your production expenses.

Another way in which cross-collateralization works applies to the performing and mechanical rights. The record company may agree to include your own original material on the record but will want an assignment of your royalties from these two sources as a way of further guaranteeing the repayment of the production expenses. These and other devices in cross-collateralization should be carefully reviewed by you and your lawyer.

The next trap for the unwary is in the area of options. The record company will spend a lot of money promoting the first album by a performer. Naturally, they will want to secure the rights to any further album. The recording agreement may well include an obligation by the performer to provide the record company with the masters for two or more albums in any year. The record company pays the expenses of any recording session and recoups them out of subsequent records. As a performer, you would be paid scale for these additional production sessions. That's fine. But what if the record company does not release any of the additional sessions? What if they don't even have the obligation to have a session but still have the option to all of your future recordings? Make sure you understand any option that you grant in a recording contract.

3. A word of caution

Most bands want to record. They jump at the first opportunity that comes into their hands. Even though their attorney, their accountant, and their manager may recommend against a recording contract, the band itself, driven by the desire to record and make a name for themselves, may push forward.

Don't be blinded by stars in your eyes about recording contracts. It may be the wrong company or the wrong time. It may, quite simply, be the wrong contract. You may end up further behind financially than you were before you started. Just because you get your name on an album, or a single, doesn't mean you're going to get a lot of financial reward.

Don't rush into a recording contract without carefully considering the advice of your manager, lawyer, and accountant. Don't let the glitter distract you from basic business considerations. It doesn't make much sense to throw away a good career and good potential for an ego trip. You might have a nice LP to put on the wall or display to your friends, but that doesn't pay the rent.

e. FINANCIAL CONSIDERATIONS OF RECORDING

Earlier in this book we talked of various ways in which money flows to songwriters and performers from their music. If you are making a record, it is important to understand how these various payments will, or will not, come to you.

First, let us assume that you did not write the music that is on the record. All songs on the record were written by others, and are covers. This means that the sole benefit you derive from the record is from its actual sale — nothing else. The number of times the record is played over the radio, in night clubs, bars, taverns, or any other source does not affect the return to you. You are simply the performer and, as such, derive your income solely from the record company and its contract with you.

You must look carefully at your recording contract. Is the royalty payable to you based on the wholesale cost of the record, or its recommended retail cost? This can make a substantial difference; if based on wholesale, the rate should be almost double a retail-based royalty. Does it include those records that are given away by record clubs or as promotional aids by the record company? If the record company gives a radio station a copy of your record, that might be great to get air time, but under most contracts it will not put a cent in your pocket. Look carefully at the contract between you and the recording company. What terms are used and, more particularly, what definitions are used? Do not assume that every copy of your record will actually return a royalty to you.

In some instances, the number of free records a company can give out without paying you a royalty is defined in the agreement; 15% seems to be the norm. But if there is no limitation, they can give away as many as they want. Your royalties will be reduced simply by the number of records given away free.

A reasonable reserve is normally also included in the agreement to cover record returns. It is usually expressed as a percentage which is deducted from the total number of records sold. While a formal accounting in the later stages may result in some of this money coming in to you, the record company will normally hold money back pending all future developments. Most agreements use the suggested retail price of the record as the base price on which to calculate royalties. Some agreements do provide for wholesale cost in which case, normally, the royalty percentage is increased. But you have to look a little closer at the contract. Remember those pictures that were taken of you just before the record was released? Remember how pleased you were when you saw your face on the cover of the album? The neat graphics? Everything else? Well, the cost has to come from somewhere, and at this stage it is coming from you.

Assuming you are being paid a royalty on the retail price of the record, you will probably find a packaging allowance buried somewhere in your recording contract. This is normally reduced to a percentage. In most cases this percentage is, once again, 15%. Assuming your record sells for $10.00 retail, this percentage calculation reduces the cost of the record (at least insofar as your royalties are concerned) to $8.50.

Further provisions in recording contracts generally reduce the royalty to nothing on records sold at discount, or those that are remaindered because there is simply no market for the product. Whether or not your record will be remaindered depends on how successful it is, or how eager the record company is to discount the LP.

Given the number of records pressed and the price your royalty is based upon, you can estimate the total possible royalties payable to you. If you calculate royalties on sales of 150,000 records through a normal recording contract, you will likely find that the performer does not make *any* money at all after costs are paid and promotional records are accounted for.

Although this may seem unfair, there is a lot to be said on the other side of the equation. Record companies point out that it costs a substantial amount of money — $200,000 or more — to produce, package, and sell a record.

Double that to $400,000 to include promotion and you have a more realistic number. Even for a major label, that is a big investment. It is also a high-risk business. Out of all the records produced, many do not sell sufficient quantity to recoup the expenses, either for you or the record company. At least, that is what the record companies say.

If your record sells well, but not well enough to pay back all the expenses that are recoupable by the record company from your royalties, you should not be liable for the difference. If you are dealing with a reputable record company, these costs will only be recoupable from your royalties; if the royalties are not sufficient, you don't have to pay back the balance. With a less reputable record company, you may have to pay back these expenses from other income. This once again points out the necessity of reviewing your recording contract with your advisors (manager, lawyer, and accountant) before you sign, and not after. It could save you a lot of money.

f. OPTIONS

Because of the investment needed to break in a new act, and the high risk factor in recording, most recording contracts will demand from you an option for future recordings. This is another way the record company has of trying to recoup its investment in you. Obviously, they think you have talent, or they would not have signed you in the first place. They have expended a lot of money on you trying to promote the initial record but it just hasn't clicked. The next one might. Therefore you can expect to find an option in your contract for further recordings over a number of years. Normally, the time of these further recordings depends upon the record company. When they call, you have to answer. Only rarely in today's market does the first record click and return all expenses. Chances are they are looking at a long-term relationship which is covered by the option. The option and its conditions must be carefully checked by you and your advisors before you sign a recording contract.

g. FURTHER OBLIGATIONS AND OPPORTUNITIES

It would be nice if all you had to do was cut a record and leave it there. Unfortunately much more is involved when you get to promotion, so you need to be prepared. This is where your manager, the talent agency, the recording company, and all the other people involved in your career get together and make things happen. Promotion is the key word at all times. (See chapter 19 for information on doing your own promo kit.)

Videos have now become very popular. Everybody wants to make one. But who is going to pay for it? Does your record company pay for the video as part of its cost? Chances are you will find that these costs are recoupable against your royalties as well.

The record company has to get your permission to use your name and picture in promoting any record. This right is given to them in the recording contract. They will also have the right to determine the photographer, the time of any photo sessions, etc. They may pay your expenses to and from any photo sessions. They may also insist that you make yourself available for promotional tours, concerts, and the like. Although the effect of tours has diminished somewhat in the past several years, there is little doubt that a tour by the band after making a record will enhance the saleability of the record.

Record companies will also promote the record through their normal distribution channels. They promote both with record stores and with radio stations. The theory is that the more the song is played on radio, the more popular the record will be, and the more copies will be sold. The more records are sold in the stores, the more the radio stations will play it. If you go on radio or on television, more people will be interested in buying the record. The more people who buy the record, the greater the chance your concerts will be successful. And from the higher attendance at the concerts, more people will buy your record. All of which means that the higher the sales of your first record, the easier it is to sell your second, when the whole promotional cycle starts again. If you get a hit, then and only then does the full world of the music business open up for you. The more hits you have, the more clout you have to deal with all of the people mentioned in this book. New worlds start to open up as well. Product endorsement of dolls, T-shirts and a million other items sold with your name or your band's name on them means increased income.

Suddenly, if things work well, you are on the top of the pyramid. Now people are coming to *you* with songs that they want *you* to record. Now people are asking *you* to do a concert (indeed, even begging you to do a concert) instead of the other way around.

h. PRIVATE PRESSING

There is no reason why you cannot make a record when you have no producer, recording company, or publisher. You can still make your own recording, sell it, and perhaps augment your income by doing so.

The key difference is, of course, that you pay all the costs of the record as you are doing it. The degree of professional help you hire will add to the costs of your record. But you can, if you really try, produce a record for very low cost and sell it from the trunk of your car at a profit.

Let's say, as a performer, that you have been successful in one city. In fact, you may even have become a "regular" at a particular bar or nightclub. Some of the patrons of that establishment will want to hear you not just in a bar, but at home as well. If you think this is the case, you may consider looking into the production of your own record under your own label and making that record available to your audience and local radio stations as well. A record like this may enhance your ability to find employment in other establishments and could lead to a recording contract with a major recording company down the road.

This means you have to wear a number of hats. First, go over all your materials and select the best. You can simplify the process if you use your own material rather than cover versions. If you use a cover version, you will have to pay the mechanical royalties to the writer of the song; if you use only your own material, this is not a problem. You will also have to form your own publishing company, which must be affiliated with the same performing rights organization as you are.

Next, you have to find a place to record your material. This means contracting with a recording studio and trying to work out the best possible deal for the use of their equipment and facilities. Many studios offer lower rates after normal business hours. Or you may even have a friend who has a good enough studio in the basement to use for this type of record. You may even wish to build one of your own. Look at the costs involved, try to reduce them as much as possible, and then try to reduce them once again.

You don't need a professional producer or the elaborate techniques now used in the recording business. Try to cut out as many of these frills as possible. Remember that most records made prior to 1964 were made with equipment not much more elaborate than your own home portable tape recorder. You will not be able to get a really top quality professional sound, but you will probably get a recording that you can sell to the members of your audience.

Contact record pressing companies in your area. Find out how much they will charge to take your tape and transfer onto vinyl. Check out the cost of packaging, the cost of printing labels, and all the other costs that will be incurred. After you find out all the costs associated with the production of your own record and feel that your entertainment income can cover this cost, you have to arrive at another decision. Will your audience buy the record? Only you can tell, and in many instances, your decision will be based on a gut reaction.

You could start out with a run of 2,000 to 5,000 copies. You will have to pay all costs in advance, but you get income back when you sell a record to a member of your audience. Consider it carefully and look at some books that tell you how to do it (see Bibliography).

19

PROMO KITS AND PUBLICITY

You could be the best band in the world and if all you want to do is play together, this may be quite all right. But if you want more — if you want engagements and potentially even a recording contract — you have to get out and hustle.

This basically involves promoting your band. As with many things in the music business, the object of the exercise is to have someone hear you who thinks you are good. Hopefully, that someone will be in a position where he or she can help you further your career.

The basic tools used in the recording business for publicity are twofold — the promo kit and the demo tape. The demo tape actually forms part of the promo kit, although it may function independently. The promo kit is aimed directly at providing publicity for your band when you need it.

a. WHAT GOES INTO YOUR PROMO KIT

Promo kits take a variety of forms. The better produced and better designed your promo kit is, the better it will assist you in gaining publicity and engagements for your group. Although many of the elements of the promo kit can be prepared by amateurs, nothing beats a good professional job. The preparation of your promo kit will introduce you to a number of other skills involved in the music business.

Your promo kit will normally take the form of a folder, and the folder should be designed to enhance and embellish your reputation. The type of material used for the cover, the printing, the design, and all other aspects of the cover should reflect your group. If you are into hard rock, a soft pastel color is definitely out of place. A solo female performer may well use a somewhat discreet cover for her promo kit; a hard rock band would probably be more daring in their cover design. If you happen to have a friend who knows advertising or print design, you might ask for assistance. If not, look in the Yellow Pages under commercial artists, advertising, or other similar headings. Shop around for the best work for the best price.

An essential part of the cover design of your promo kit will be the band's logo, if you choose to use one. Even the style of script associated with your band's name should be chosen with an eye to its advertising appeal. Although commercial artists and advertising professionals are expensive, the final product will undoubtedly be better than an amateur job by the school art class.

If your cover contains a logo for the band, the logo should be repeated on all other publicity material in the promo kit. This reinforces the design motif and implants the name of the band and its logo on whoever glances through the promo kit.

The promo kit will also contain biographies of all members of the band, and the band itself. These biographies generally stress the musical abilities of the band members, the other bands they have played with, and so on. They will also list your successes. If you have been booked at one engagement, received rave reviews, and were "held over" with packed houses all the way, this information will form part of your "musical biography."

No one really wants to know that you won the 100 yard dash in your high school track and field meet. They do want to know what you have done in music and how successful you have been. If each member of the band has played with other groups, this is important, particularly if those groups have been successful on the local scene. For example, "Mike was a member of *Rare Books* until the band broke up in 1984. While it was performing, *Rare Books* sold out in performances at various night clubs in our city, including The Kingdom, Commercial Potential, and The Law Forum." Material on the members of the band and their past successes in music are particularly relevant if the band itself is new.

It may be that a member of the band or a friend is capable of doing a write-up for you for free. If not, check around with other bands and get a reference to a good publicist. This is a person who, for a fee, will write up the history of the band and the band biographies in a presentable and professional fashion.

The next ingredient of a promo kit (particularly those aimed at gaining additional engagements) is a list of the music you play. If you are a Top 40 group, this should be stressed; include your current "play list" for reference. Your publicist will review this list and may emphasize new hits and current material. One or two pages outlining the current material you are performing will be sufficient.

How you choose to feature your original material is a somewhat different proposition. If the band has had some success with original material, reflect this success in the list of songs and the band's biography. However, for a new band, perhaps the worst thing you can do is include a list of material that is *all* original — no one knows whether it is good or bad, and many club owners will not be willing to take a chance to find out. Review the list of materials included in your promo kit with your agent and manager. As they will be more familiar with the music marketplace, accept their guidance in this area.

Promo kits normally also include copies of all reviews that were favorable to the band or its members. Even if it is just a local paper from a small town, put it in. The more reviews you can add, the better. However, use your discretion — no one wants to receive a promo kit with 300 pages of reviews. Seek the advice of your publicist, manager and agent.

b. YOUR PHOTOGRAPHER

Everyone can take pictures. Unfortunately, some people take better pictures than others. The people who take excellent pictures are normally professional photographers who charge for their work.

Your promo kit should contain perhaps five or six "publicity stills," showing the band or even the solo performer.

People want to know what you look like before they hire you. You can convey much of the "mood" of the band simply by the nature of the publicity photos in your promo kit. As with the list of your music, you can use the photos to reflect the mood or feeling the band wishes to create.

Photographers use a number of different physical props for publicity photos. Dark alleyways, stage doorways, staircases, and others all have their place. You will probably find, however, that many of these are simply "too busy" for day-to-day use, particularly if posters are being printed using your photos. Include a few different types — some with busy backgrounds, others with simple white backdrops. Remember that some of these photos may appear on posters. You want a clear sharp image that conveys the mood of the band to your potential audience.

Your photographer, manager, agent, and probably everybody in the band will want to choose the best photos. A professional photographer will normally offer you quite a number of options and choices. You should decide which are going to be printed up for the promo kit.

A photographer is expensive. Ask the photographer what his or her rates are before you proceed. If you want additional copies of the photographs (as is quite likely), ask if there is a special rate. You will normally find that you can get a better rate per photograph if you order a large number. Also, verify with the photographer that the photographs will be used for publicity purposes and that proper professional credit for the photos will be given.

c. THE DEMO TAPE

The last ingredient of your promo kit will be a copy of your demo tape. Try and include the four best songs that the band presents. This promo tape does not *have* to be recorded in a professional studio. You may even include some tapes of actual live performances if they are of good enough quality and show the band performing at its best. One performer's promo tape even included comments from the audience — a daring but effective touch.

d. PROMO KIT VARIATIONS

A promo kit should be tailored to the specific job you want it to do. If you are seeking work as a performer, the kit should be geared to your skills as a performer. If you are promoting your work as a songwriter, your promo kit will stress the type of material you have written in the past, and the cover versions made. Your demo tape will, of course, be substantially different than a performer's demo tape. In each case, let the professionals around you assist you to target the demo tape for its specific use.

e. CIRCULATION OF THE PROMO KIT

If one or more members of the band are actively looking for work for the band, they should be armed with copies of the promo kit. Get out and meet the managers of the clubs, pubs, nightspots, and other places where live music is played. Present each of these people with a copy of your promo kit. Make sure your promo kit is in the hands of your talent agency and your manager. In other words, once you have gone to all the time and effort of making a good promo kit, get it out there and working for you. Although personal contact is best, use the mail if that is the only route open to you.

Your promo kit is really one large business card. Because of the nature of the business, it includes more items. But you have to give plenty of information about yourself (particularly in the early stages) to secure engagements and further work.

20

CONCLUSION

Success in the music business can mean a number of things. Some view success as the personal feeling they achieve by simply performing in front of an audience. Others are happy playing weekend engagements to pick up a little bit of extra cash. Some want a part-time hobby; still others will only be satisfied with the top of the ladder and a hit.

Only you can determine what you want from the music business and how you will achieve your success. Regardless of your goal, the business techniques referred to in this book should help you on your way.

MAILING ADDRESSES FOR THE MUSIC BUSINESS

a. COPYRIGHT OFFICES

1. Canada

The Commissioner of Patents
The Copyright Office
Ottawa-Hull, Canada
K1A 0C9

2. U.S.A.

U.S. Copyright Office
Library of Congress
Washington, D.C.   20559

b. UNIONS AND GUILDS

1. Canada

American Federation of Musicians of the United States
  and Canada
86 Overlea Boulevard
Suite 404
Toronto, Ontario
M4H 1C6

Alliance of Canadian Cinema, Television, and
  Radio Artists (ACTRA)
2239 Yonge Street
Toronto, Ontario
M45 2B5

2. U.S.A.

American Federation of Musicians of the United States
  and Canada
1500 Broadway
New York, New York   10036

American Federation of Television and
  Radio Artists (AFTRA)
1350 Avenue of the Americas
New York, New York   10019

American Guild of Authors and Composers
  (The Songwriters' Guild)
40 West 57th Street
New York, New York   10019

American Guild of Musical Artists (AGMA)
1841 Broadway
New York, New York   10036

American Guild of Variety Artists (AGVA)
1540 Broadway
New York, New York   10036

Composers, and Lyricists' Guild of America
6565 Sunset Boulevard
Los Angeles, California   90028

c. PERFORMING RIGHTS ORGANIZATIONS
1. Canada

Composers, Authors, and Publishers Association
  of Canada Ltd. (CAPCAN)
1240 Bay Street
Toronto, Ontario
M5R 2C2

Performing Rights Organization of Canada Ltd.
  (PROCAN)
41 Valleybrook Drive
Don Mills, Ontario
M3B 2S6

2. U.S.A.

American Society of Composers, Authors, and
  Publishers (ASCAP)
One Lincoln Plaza
New York, New York   10023

Broadcast Music Inc.
3230 West 57th Street
New York, New York   10019

Sesac, Inc.
10 Columbus Circle
New York, New York   10019

d. MECHANICAL RIGHTS ORGANIZATIONS
1. Canada

CANAMEC (mechanical rights division of Performing
  Rights Organization of Canada Ltd.)
45 Valleybrook Drive
Don Mills, Ontario
M3B 2S6

Canadian Musical Reproduction Rights Agency Ltd.
111 Avenue Road
Toronto, Ontario
M3R 3J8

2. U.S.A.

The Harry Fox Agency
110 East 59th Street
New York, New York   10022

The American Mechanical Rights Association
250 West 57th Street
New York, New York   10017

The Copyright Service Bureau Ltd.
221 West 57th Street
New York, New York   10019

Mietus Copyright Management
527 Madison Avenue
New York, New York   10022

e. OTHER ADDRESSES
1. Canada

Carnet Canada, Division of the Canadian
   Chamber of Commerce
1080 Beaver Hall Hill
Montreal, Quebec
H2Z 1T2

or

Vancouver Board of Trade
500-1177 West Hastings Street
Vancouver, British Columbia
V6E 2K3

2. U.S.A.

American Protection Service
P.O. Box 57
Hollywood, California   90028

Songwriters' Resources and Services
6301 Hollywood Boulevard
Hollywood, California   90028

U.S. Council of the International Chamber of
  Commerce Inc.
1212 Avenue of the Americas
New York, New York   10036
or
3345 Wilshire Boulevard
Los Angeles, California   90010

BIBLIOGRAPHY

Bacon, Tony, ed. *Rock Hardware*. New York: Harmony Books, 1981.

Beverly Hills Bar Association. *Acquiring and Using Music*. Los Angeles: University of Southern California, 1962.

Burton, Gary. *The Musician's Guide to the Road*. New York: Billboard Publications, 1981

Busnar, Jean. *Careers in Music*. New York: Julian Messner, 1982.

Chapple, Steve, and Garofalo, Reebee. *Rock and Roll is Here to Pay*. New York: Nelson Hall Publishers, 1978.

Coxson, Mona. *Some Straight Talk About the Music Business*. Toronto: CM Books, 1984.

Davis, Clive. *Clive: Inside the Record Business*. New York: William Morrow and Company Inc., 1975.

Dearing, James W. *Making Money, Making Music*. Cincinnati: Writer's Digest Books, 1982.

Erickson, J. Gunnar; Hearn, Edward R.; and Holloran, Mark E. *Musician's Guide to Copyright*. New York: Charles Scribner's Sons, 1983.

Frascogna, Xavier M., and Heatherington, H. Lee. *Successful Artist Management*. New York: Billboard Publications, 1980.

Hammond, Ray. *Working at the Music Business*. Poole, Dorset, Blandord Press, 1983.

Hemphill, Paul. *The Nashville Sound*. New York: Simon & Schuster, 1970.

Huber, David A. *A Musician's Guide to the Recording Studio*. Seattle: American Institute of Music, 1984.

Karshner, Roger. *The Music Machine*. Los Angeles: Nash Publishing, 1971.

Lambert, Dennis, and Zalkind, Ronald. *Producing Hit Records*. New York: Schirmer Books, 1984.

Lindey, Alexander. *Entertainment, Publishing and the Arts (Volumes 1 to 3)*. New York: Clark Boardman Co. Ltd., 1978.

Malhuish, Martin. *Heart of Gold*. Toronto: Insight Productions Co. Ltd., 1983.

Martin, George, ed., *Making Music*. London: Pan Books Ltd., 1983.

Mills, John V. *You and the Music Business*. Toronto: CAPAC, 1983.

Monaco, Bob, and Riordan, James. *The Platinum Rainbow*. California: Swordsman Press, 1983.

Rapaport, Diane S. *How to Make and Sell Your Own Record*. New York: Quick Fox Publishing, 1981.

Rappoport, Victor D. *Making it in Music*. New Jersey: Prentice Hall, 1979.

Rogers, Kenney, and Epand, Len. *Making it with Music*. New York: Harper & Row, 1978.

Schulenberg, Richard A. *Legal Aspects of the Music Business (Volumes 1 to 6)*. San Francisco: Richard A. Schulenberg, 1980.

Selz, Thomas D., and Simensky, Melvin. *Entertainment Law: Legal Concepts and Business Practice*. Colorado Springs: Shepard's/McGraw Hill, 1983.

Shemel, Sidney, and Krasilovsky, M. William. *This Business of Music*. New York: Billboard Publications, 1979.

_____. *More About this Business of Music*. New York: Billboard Publications, 1982.

Siegal, Allen. *Breaking into the Music Business*. New York: Cherry Lane Books, 1983.

Spurgeon, C. Paul. *Copyright Law in the United States*. Toronto: CAPAC.

Stein, Howard. *Promoting Rock Concerts*. New York: Zadoc Books/Schirmar Books, 1979.

Stokes, Geoffrey. *StarMaking Machinery*. Indianapolis: Bobbs-Merrill Company, 1976.

Taubman, Joseph, ed. *The Business and Law of Music*. New York: Federal Legal Publications, 1965.

_____. *Performing Arts Management and Law*. New York: Law Arts Publishers, 1972.

Whitburn, Joel. *The Billboard Book of Top 40 Hits — 1955 to Present*. New York: Billboard Publications, 1981.

Zalkin, Ronald. *Getting Ahead in the Music Business*. New York: Schirmar Books, 1981.

CANADIAN
ORDER FORM
SELF-COUNSEL SERIES

04/85

NATIONAL TITLES:

Aids to Independence	
Advertising for Small Business	4.95
Assertiveness for Managers	8.95
Basic Accounting	5.95
Be a Better Manager	7.95
Better Book for Getting Hired	9.95
Business Guide to Effective Speaking	6.95
Business Guide to Telephone Systems	7.95
Buying (and Selling) a Small Business	6.95
Changing Your Name in Canada	3.50
Civil Rights	8.95
Collection Techniques for the Small Business	4.95
Complete Guide to Being Your Own Home Contractor	19.95
Credit, Debt, and Bankruptcy	5.95
Criminal Procedure in Canada	12.95
Design Your Own Logo	9.95
Drinking and Driving	4.50
Editing Your Newsletter	14.95
Exporting	12.50
Family Ties That Bind	7.95
Federal Incorporation and Business Guide	12.95
Financial Control for the Small Business	5.95
Financial Freedom on $5 A Day	6.95
For Sale By Owner	4.95
Franchising in Canada	5.95
Fundraising	5.50
Getting Money	14.95
Getting Sales	14.95
Getting Started	11.95
How You Too Can Make a Million . . . In the Mail Order Business	8.95
Immigrating to Canada	12.95
Immigrating to the U.S.A.	14.95
Importing	21.95
Insuring Business Risks	3.50
Landlording in Canada	12.95
Learn to Type Fast	6.50
Life Insurance for Canadians	3.50
Managing Your Office Records and Files	14.95
Media Law Handbook	6.50
Medical Law Handbook	
Mike Grenby's Money Book	5.50
Mike Grenby's Tax Tips	6.95
Mortgage and Foreclosure Handbook	5.95
Parents' Guide to Day Care	5.95
Practical Guide to Financial Management	5.95
Resort Condos	4.50
Retirement Guide for Canadians	9.95
Start and Run a Profitable Beauty Salon	14.95
Start and Run a Profitable Consulting Business	12.95
Start and Run a Profitable Craft Business	10.95
Start and Run a Profitable Home Typing Business	9.95
Start and Run a Profitable Restaurant	10.95
Start and Run a Profitable Retail Business	11.95
Start and Run a Profitable Video Store	10.95
Starting a Successful Business in Canada	12.95
Tax Law Handbook	12.95
Taxpayer Alert!	4.95
Tax Shelters	6.95
Trusts and Trust Companies	3.95
Upper Left-Hand Corner	10.95
Using the Access to Information Act	5.95
Word Processing	8.95
Working Couples	5.50
Write Right!	(Cloth) 5.95 / (Paper) 4.95

PROVINCIAL TITLES:
Please indicate which provincial edition is required.

Consumer Book
☐B.C. 7.95   ☐Ontario 6.95

Divorce Guide
□B.C. 10.95 □Alberta 9.95 □Ontario 9.95 □Man./Sask.

Employee/Employer Rights
□B.C. 6.95 □Alberta 6.95 □Ontario 5.50

Fight That Ticket
□B.C. 5.95 □Ontario 3.95

Incorporation Guide
□B.C. 14.95 □Alberta 14.95 □Ontario 14.95 □Man./Sask.

Landlord/Tenant Rights
□B.C.   □Alberta 5.50 □Ontario 6.95

Marriage & Family Law
□B.C. 7.95 □Alberta 5.95 □Ontario 7.95

Probate Guide
□B.C. 12.95 □Alberta 9.95 □Ontario 9.95

Real Estate Guide
□B.C. 7.95 □Alberta 4.95 □Ontario 6.50

Small Claims Court Guide
□B.C. 6.95 □Alberta 7.50 □Ontario 5.95

Wills
□B.C. 5.50 □Alberta 5.95 □Ontario 5.50

Wills/Probate Procedure
□Sask./Man. 4.95

PACKAGED FORMS:

Divorce
□B.C. 12.95 □Alberta 12.95 □Ontario 14.50 □Man. 8.50 □Sask.

Incorporation
□B.C. 12.95 □Alberta 11.95 □Ontario 14.95

□Man.   □Sask.   □Federal 9.95

□Minute Books 16.50

Probate
□B.C. Administration 14.95 □B.C. Probate 14.95 □Alberta 13.95 □Ontario 15.50

Sell Your Own Home
□B.C. 4.95 □Alberta 4.95 □Ontario 4.95

□Rental Form Kit (B.C., Alberta, Ontario, Sask.)   5.95

□ Have You Made Your Will?   5.95

□ If You Love Me Put It In Writing   Contract Kit   9.95

□ If You Leave Me Put It In Writing   B.C. Separation Agreement Kit 14.95

NOTE: All prices subject to change without notice.

Books are available in book and department stores, or use the order form below.
Please enclose cheque or money order (plus sales tax where applicable) or give us your
MasterCard or Visa Number (please include validation and expiry date).

(PLEASE PRINT)

Name _____

Address _____

City _____

Province _____ Postal Code _____

□ Visa/ □ MasterCard Number _____

Validation Date _____ Expiry Date _____

If order is under $20.00, add $1.00 for postage and handling.

Please send orders to:

INTERNATIONAL SELF-COUNSEL PRESS LTD.   □ Check here for free catalogue.
306 West 25th Street
North Vancouver, British Columbia
V7N 2G1

AMERICAN
ORDER FORM
SELF-COUNSEL SERIES

11/84

NATIONAL TITLES

_____ Assertiveness for Managers	8.95
_____ Basic Accounting for the Small Business	5.95
_____ Be a Better Manager	7.95
_____ Business Guide to Effective Speaking	6.95
_____ Business Guide to Telephone Systems	7.95
_____ Buying (and Selling) a Small Business	6.95
_____ Collection Techniques for the Small Business	4.95
_____ Design Your Own Logo	
_____ Exporting from the U.S.A.	12.95
_____ Family Ties That Bind	7.95
_____ Financial Control for the Small Business	5.50
_____ Financial Freedom on $5 A Day	6.95
_____ Fundraising for Non-Profit Groups	5.50
_____ Franchising in the U.S.	5.95
_____ Getting Sales	14.95
_____ How You Too Can Make a Million . . . In the Mail Order Business	8.95
_____ Immigrating to Canada	12.95
_____ Immigrating to the U.S.A.	14.95
_____ Learn to Type Fast	6.50
_____ The Money Spinner	14.95
_____ Parents' Guide to Day Care	5.95
_____ Practical Guide to Financial Management	5.95
_____ Resort Condos and Time Sharing	4.50
_____ Retirement in the Pacific Northwest	4.95
_____ Start and Run a Profitable Beauty Salon	14.95
_____ Start and Run a Profitable Craft Business	10.95
_____ Start and Run a Profitable Home Typing Business	9.95
_____ Start and Run a Profitable Restaurant	10.95
_____ Start and Run a Profitable Retail Business	11.95
_____ Start and Run a Profitable Video Store	10.95
_____ Starting a Successful Business on West Coast	12.95
_____ Upper Left-Hand Corner	10.95
_____ You and the Police	3.50
_____ Word Processing	5.50
_____ Working Couples	4.50

STATE TITLES
Please indicate which state edition is required.

_____ Divorce Guide
    ☐ Washington (with forms) 12.95   ☐ Oregon 11.95

_____ Employee/Employer Rights
    ☐ Washington 5.50

_____ Incorporation and Business Guide
    ☐ Washington   ☐ Oregon 11.95

_____ Landlord/Tenant Rights
☐ Washington 5.95 ☐ Oregon 6.95

_____ Marriage and Family Law
☐ Washington 4.50 ☐ Oregon 4.95

_____ Probate Guide
☐ Washington 9.95

_____ Real Estate Buying/Selling Guide
☐ Washington 5.95 ☐ Oregon 3.95

_____ Small Claims Court
☐ Washington 4.50

_____ Wills
☐ Washington   ☐ Oregon 5.95

PACKAGED FORMS

_____ Divorce
☐ Oregon Set A (Petitioner) 12.95
☐ Oregon Set B (Co-Petitioners) 12.95

_____ If You Love Me — Put It In Writing 7.95

_____ Incorporation
☐ Washington 12.95 ☐ Oregon 10.50

_____ Probate
☐ Washington 6.50

_____ Will and Estate Planning Kit 4.95

All prices subject to change without notice.

Please send orders to:

SELF-COUNSEL PRESS INC.
1303 N. Northgate Way
Seattle, Washington 98133

☐ Check here for free catalog

(PLEASE PRINT)

NAME _____

ADDRESS _____

CITY _____

STATE _____

ZIP CODE _____

Check or Money Order enclosed ☐

If order is under $20.00, add $1.50 for postage and handling.